Lily, Oh Lily

Lily, Oh Lily

SEARCHING FOR A NAZI GHOST

Jeffrey Paparoa Holman

CANTERBURY UNIVERSITY PRESS

UNIVERSITY OF
CANTERBURY
Te Whare Wānanga o Waitaha
CHRISTCHURCH NEW ZEALAND

First published in 2024 by
CANTERBURY UNIVERSITY PRESS
University of Canterbury
Private Bag 4800, Christchurch
New Zealand

Text copyright © 2024 Jeffrey Paparoa Holman
The moral right of the author has been asserted

Illustrations © the author or as attributed

Every effort has been made to trace and acknowledge owners of copyright material. If notified of any errors or omissions the publisher will be pleased to rectify them at the earliest opportunity.

ISBN 978-1-98-850347-9

A catalogue record for this book is available from the
National Library of New Zealand.

This book is copyright. Except for the purpose of fair review, no part may be stored or transmitted in any form or by any means, electronic or mechanical, including recording or storage in any information retrieval system, without permission in writing from the publishers. No reproduction may be made, whether by photocopying or by any other means, unless a licence has been obtained from the publisher or its agent.

Editor: Gillian Tewsley
Book design and layout: Katrina Duncan
Author photo: Romain Fiasson (2013)

Front cover images: Lilian Edith (Lily) Hasenburg, passport photo, 1934. ANCESTRY.COM, PUBLIC DOMAIN. Hitler is greeted by the masses as he is driven through the crowd, Germany, c.1936. HERITAGE IMAGE PARTNERSHIP LTD/ALAMY STOCK PHOTO
Image on page 2: Lily Hasenburg (Bywater). FAMILY ALBUM

Printed in China through Asia Pacific Offset

To:

Patrick Evans, writer, teacher, mentor, friend

Nanny – Eunice Winifred Airey (née Bywater)

Konrad und Gaby Kutt, meine wunderbar Berliner Gastgeber

Contents

Foreword	9
Family Tree	13
In the Beginning, the Dead	17

HOME

One Listening to Nanny Eunice	21
Two Meeting the Remarkable Bywaters	33
Three Cousin Robin and the Jewish Husband	48
Four Nanny's Address Book and Mormon Helpers	52

AWAY

Five I Land in Berlin	67
Six Germany is My Teacher	73
Seven Passing German at the Goethe-Institut	88
Eight Encounters in London Fields	93
Nine Manuel is My Hamburg Genealogist	101
Ten Grunewald and the Leaping Hare	109
Eleven Taking Old Glory Back to Dresden	114
Twelve Certificates of Birth and Death	126
Thirteen Victor Culture and Colonial Amnesia	132
Fourteen English Lily in a German War	140
Fifteen Great-uncle Uly and the Gestapo	144
Sixteen Lily is Interned on the Isle of Man	154
Seventeen Looking into the Graves	164
Eighteen From the Hotel Adlon to Kensal Green	172

HOME

Coda The Real Story of the Book	181
Postscript Germany After 1945	184
Notes	191
Bibliography	196
Mihimihi/Acknowledgements	198

Foreword

Jeffrey's generation of baby-boomers, so-called, were born into the domestic wreckage of the Second World War and the promise of a land war in Asia as their own special destiny. They grew to know of damaged and missing parents, uncles, cousins and especially (as this book tells us) aunts, and were often taught by angry, broken men with PTSD. They were forced to find their own place in this brave new world, to work out the new rules, to make peace with the deal they'd been given: so many opportunities 'out there', but so much pain around us, too, which young people were never allowed to talk about. After all, the baby-boomers were the lucky generation.

All these experiences underwrite Jeffrey's extraordinarily committed life-writing project: essentially, to start the talk, to tell the tales, to begin to understand and establish that particular postwar world as something that can be better known, better understood, and better talked about. He tells the tales. At first, for him, this has meant going into the past, writing about early Pākehā ethnography and absorbing te reo and tikanga Māori to make a place to stand in, at the bicultural meeting-point of a postwar Aotearoa, a New Zealand where traditional European values become a lived understanding of te ao Māori. This understanding informs his poetry as it has his life, bringing a perspective to Pākehā experience different from that of many other writers – a sense of a particular life intricated in all his writing, from his longer projects, like the Blackball Bridge sonnets, to his tiny poem 'Pīwakawaka', where a single moment comes to life in a few words.

Lily, Oh Lily is part of another kind of confrontation with the nagging of our inherited silences, a project of self-understanding and self-establishment, which meticulously places the author in the larger flows of history. In this, it is a sequel to *The Lost Pilot*, 2013, where Jeffrey records his extraordinary plunge into the extreme otherness of Japanese life and culture to find the family of a young Japanese kamikaze pilot. This man – youth – all but obliterated Jeffrey's father in an attack on the carrier HMS *Illustrious*, off the Sakishima islands in 1945 – and, logically, his father's son, who is writing the words on the page that tell of his painstaking search. A non-Japanese speaker with no experience in driving on the right – no problem: let's hire a car and drive off alone into a completely alien culture and see what we find!

Lily, Oh Lily involves the same dogged trudge through the scenes-of-the-crime, through further remnants of the Second World War in which to find clues, links, ideas, proof – to find a story, which is the story of that search. *Lily, Oh Lily* is a thriller, a search for a particular person caught in the events of Nazi Germany – not a whodunnit, but a where-is-she. It becomes a metafiction, a parable of the writing process which shows us what happens before fiction and as we strive to make it, living on the border between the memories of a lived life and the beginnings of the writing of a story. It gives us the processes which cause us to write – memory, obsession, remembering, misremembering, the power of the imagination not to let things go, the sheer bloodiness and horror of what might supply the written page. It explores the remnants of Nazism, how a particular history affects the lives of the little people, like the mysterious aunt, about whom almost nothing is known except that she chose to live in Nazi Germany when Hitler was there. In this book, she becomes Hitchcock's MacGuffin, the mysterious, must-be-found figure who leads us through the text – and who can never be found, because what matters is the journey. In another sense, of course, she 'is' the story, a real figure who comes in and out of focus, who flickers into life for us from time to time, who gives meaning to the fiction of memory by showing us where she lived, who she met, who she knew and what happened to them. In the failure of her retrieval Jeffrey has created the ghost of an actual individual, half-known, almost there, like so many humans caught up in that terrible time in our history. And in this one.

Patrick Evans
February 2024

A family is a jigsaw with many missing pieces

Wozu Dichter in dürftiger Zeit?
(What use are poets in wretched times?)
— FRIEDRICH HÖLDERLIN, 'BREAD AND WINE', 1801

And I realise writing this that memory is as much an act of creation as it is of testimony, and that one without the other is a tree without its trunk, wings without a bird, a book without its story.
— RICHARD FLANAGAN, *QUESTION 7*

Where we begin: Bywaters all, Lily, Ulysses, Hector (rear), Peter Daniel, Mary and Eunice. From the Welsh front row, I have emerged; from the mysterious backs, my writing. Looking at them closely, as always, do they come nearer, or remain out of reach? FAMILY ALBUM

Family Tree

There are two Lilian/Lillians in this family: my subject, my great-aunt Lilian; and my aunt Lillian Mitchell, my mother's older sister. My grandmother, in my recall, always referred to her sister as 'Lily', so she is named Lily here in this account of her life. The only exception is when official documents are cited, and context makes obvious, Lilian is Lily.

My grandmother, Eunice Airey (née Bywater), will appear in the story as Nanny.

Overleaf: Bywater family tree showing characters who appear in the text.

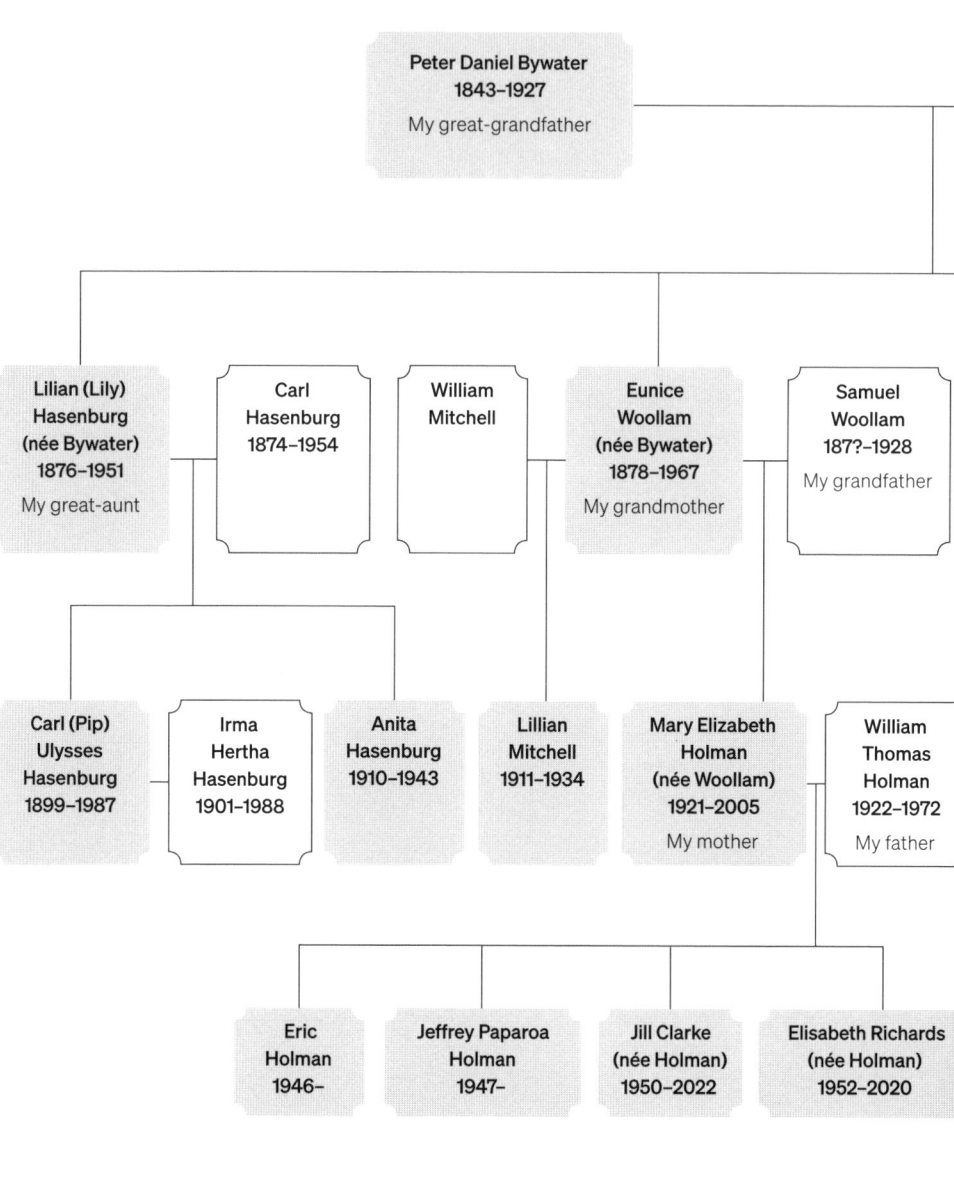

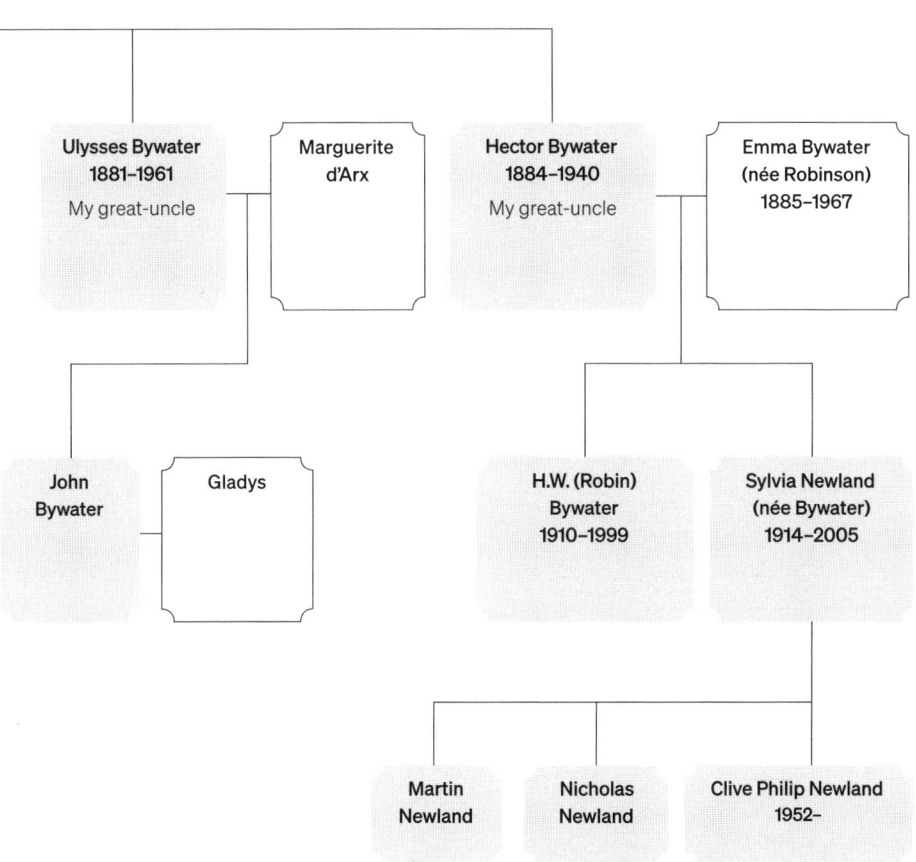

In the Beginning, the Dead

> I spent my childhood with [my grandfather], because my mother was too busy and my father was a prisoner of war. I learned everything from him and still think of him every day. You see, behind all of us who are living there are the dead. In fact they are here coexisting with us, but we don't see them. We have unlearned the ability to see them.
> — W.G. 'MAX' SEBALD [1]

The shadow of an unexplained Germany and the Germans hangs over my family like a mute muse, calling me to explain Germania's presence from the shreds of evidence that written and spoken memories have left to me. The dead are the most interesting people I have ever interviewed. They have no volition, no rights, no slick publicists, and present as stone idols to a Kipling trooper. Impassively, they refuse me: yet always they leave a few small clues – willed or not – which makes them irresistible. They never surrender their mysterious presence-in-absence, never wholly die, at least to the one who cares for their accounts of life, those of us still on this side of where they once were, breathing in the light – like you and like me.

Sitting at my desk, having crunched my way through an apple, it occurs to me that my forebears, on a day in time, did something similar, disposed of the core and went on with their day. That thought holds a mirror to an obsessive quest, my pursuit of the dead in my family tree, the fallen fruit. Is it the otherness of their lives I'm looking for, or the sameness: that they lived and died in another time, yet slept, woke, ate, worked, played, felt hope and fear, just as I sit here, still drawing breath?

Or is it possibly the otherness of their deaths that draws me in, the fact they have an alien nature I cannot yet share, but one day will – if not today, next week or next month, then certainly in an oncoming year? One thing is certain about them: as the dead, they are a tribe we belong to but cannot yet join, until life vanishes in a breath. Their totality, their completeness, their story-like resolution is something that awaits us, unconsciously invited, studiously avoided. When death comes, when the dead know their end at last, they slam their door in the faces of the living. We want to know the way the story ends, yet shrink back from joining them, from finding out how.

Next door and far away, like our loved ones and our neighbours, the dead bring us back to our lives as the living. They remind us we are time-governed, time-limited, but in the act of remembrance, we can be outside of time, where they are not yet wholly dead, because not forgotten. This is the greatest gift of writing: when, at three generations, oral memories may die, yet the written dead continue in this world, but only as sharply, as truly, as they have been recalled and recorded. Their gift has been the bringing of us into the world; ours can be to keep them here while no longer beside us in the flesh. Tihei mauri ora! They call, speak to us, rising within.

HOME

ONE

Listening to Nanny Eunice

SOMETIME IN MY FIFTEENTH YEAR, IN BLACKBALL, UNDER THE impression that to be really intelligent I had to read important-sounding books, I began to order titles from a Penguin Books catalogue, got from who-knows-where, works by Nietzsche – along with other weirdos whose names I could hardly spell. You could not get such things from my local bookshop; they had to be ordered from the city, Christchurch.

Bad move. I should have stuck to things I really enjoyed, like Biggles books, war comics and *Flight* magazines, all devoured in answer to my hunger to fly. I needed that stuff; I surely did not need, at that moment in my life, to be trying to make sense of *Thus Spoke Zarathustra* or *The Gay Science* (that title had no echo of man love back then – at least, not to me). I had a friend, Jim Hopkins, who visited from the city; Jim convinced me that it was cool to read such greats as Dostoyevsky, and that it was high time for me to widen my horizons. With feelings of inferiority running hot, I bought into his argument and tried self-improvement by way of reading great literature.

I think it gave me a lasting kind of constipation whereby I was blocked from consuming what I liked and enjoyed, instead wading into what was supposed to be good for me. No disrespect to the giants of Western literature, but back then my needs were more humble. How could I get airborne and keep on fighting the Battle of Britain in my trusty Hawker Hurricane, flinging myself and my deadly craft at the black crosses of the oncoming Nazi bombers, Tally-ho, chaps! Reading, to me at that time, was a way of controlling my crazy world, reducing reality to a place where I was in charge and the bullies had better look out. Now I had eight .303 machine guns to defend my country, to become the kind of hero my blood-soaked war comics promised I could be: so powerful, much feared, admired, unbeaten.

At that age, I wanted to be a normal fifteen-year-old, in no hurry for all the adult stuff to arrive, as surely it would. I'd had enough of adulthood in what I could see around me: unhappy, frustrated parents under our roof and under the roofs of other kids I knew. I loved music – the way it made me feel, the words, the clever poetry of pop, silly songs, love songs, the stuff on the radio, at a time when none of us had radiograms, or television. Sound was king, radio the music. I made up in my head whatever pictures were needed, in my own time and space. That was me, Douglas Bader's wingman, singing along with Roy Orbison, studying *Famous Fighters of the Second World War* by William Green, making guns to play war with the other kids, all by now noticeably younger than me. My peers were leaving school, getting jobs and buying motorbikes. I have no shame in confessing to being a very late developer: I had about as much use then for a BSA Scrambler as for Franz Kafka and his weird *Castle*. All that could wait, and it did – but not for long.

At least until one summer holiday, when my city friend Jim turned up after Christmas to stay for a couple of weeks. He may have been this cool, sophisticated townie compared to me, but he loved our West Coast coalmining town with its bush shoulders, orchards to raid, and deep, wide rivers where eels could be speared. He always brought his latest book. This one, with its khaki and grey cover, grabbed my attention: *The First World War: An Illustrated History* by A.J.P. Taylor. On the cover, carnage: dead horses, broken gun carriages, walking wounded in a desert of blasted, broken trees. On the back, two riders

– Kaiser Wilhelm II and his English cousin, King George V – arrayed as if for battle, to inspect all the doomed troops. A series of powerful black and white photos, often with sarcastic and bitter comments ('Lloyd George casts an expert eye over munitions girls'), began to make history come alive and lift off the page. My Nanny Eunice, who lived with us, had worked in just such a place; I had seen this picture of her in the family album she would sometimes open. There she was in her brown tunic and red striped bonnet, at war.

'What recall after all these years,' you may be thinking – but no, not at all. I still have my copy of Taylor's book, a first edition, 1963, open before me, having just slid it off the shelf. I sit here now, inhaling its odour of age and authority. The book was signed by me, as owner, with my Parker 45 fountain pen – another acquisition I had come to covet after seeing Jim with one. There I am, in my schoolboy hand – '*J. Holman, Main Rd., Blackball*' – imprinting my presence in time itself. I did not know this then, but it would slowly come true: the book was changing my life. In that moment I was ripe to grow up a little; it only took the right card of chance, dealt with no aim, to land on my table. This cascade of horrors, unfolding a death march of images, made it impossible to avoid the implications of my Battle of Britain air ace fantasy. This was the first book I had ever seen to show me real war.

Now it is 2023, the new year has just come in; it is near on sixty years ago that Taylor's book came into my life. At no time since have I quite escaped its lessons, warnings that walked off the pages into my very bones, graven by the black-and-white ghosts of half-buried dead soldiers jack-knifed in trench walls; of German women scavenging for food in Berlin. Their deaths, their despair seeped into my bedroom, into my bed where I read at night before dropping asleep, innocence sloughed off in the face of horror. No wonder at fifteen I was still wetting the bed.

Somewhere in Germany, unknown to me then, my grandmother's sister, my great-aunt Lily Bywater, married to German rubber dealer Carl Hasenburg from Hamburg, had lived during the First World War. What was that like for her? She was an Englishwoman in Germany, at war with her country of birth, while her sister, soon to become a supervisor in a shell factory at Quedgeley in Gloucestershire, was to be engaged in the production of deadly munitions to be rained on Germany's armies – on Lily and her adoptive fellow citizens. How did she deal with that? How did Lily's German friends and neighbours begin to look upon her, she now belonging to the enemy tribe? Taylor's book had images of hungry German children, fed in the streets from soup kitchens on wheels. There were also photographs that told of things to come: 'undefeated' German troops marching home with flowers in their helmets, a crop of poison in their ranks, deep in their hearts, seeding the lie they had been 'stabbed in the back' – by traitors. 'When Germans referred to "peacetime" after 1918, it was not to the era in which they were actually living, but to the period before the Great War had begun. Germany failed to make the transition from wartime back to peacetime, after 1918. Instead, it remained on a continued war footing; at war with itself and at war with the rest of the world …'.[1] This was the Dolchstoßlegende, of a Germany betrayed by Jews, socialists and republican politicians, a lie that was embraced by thousands of embittered veterans, most notably, for the future of Europe, by one German soldier in particular – Adolf Hitler.

I recall vividly the photo on page 148, captioned by Taylor, 'The wicked Hun': in fact, it was a German prisoner taken at Passchendaele, looking lost, quite bereft. Once again, the author was indulging in sarcasm and irony; the image showed a seemingly thoughtful, bespectacled young man, his tunic dishevelled, his resigned expression shadowed with fatigue, crowned with what seemed to be an outsized Stahlhelm, the standard German army helmet. He looks neither wicked nor dangerous; more, bewildered and exhausted, than a man having anything to do with evil or power.

Yet somehow, both through being related by blood to my Nanny, and through the effect of these wartime black-and-white images, the human cost of such a conflict to the teenage war-comic addict I then was had already triggered a hunger to know more. Late in my life, these impulses led me to seek out the story of one whose tale deserves telling: my great-aunt Lily Hasenburg, née Bywater. All this because

Illustration of the Dolchstoßlegende, Austrian postcard, 1919.
PUBLIC DOMAIN

of a comment she had made to my Nanny in 1934, and long remembered, to be recalled and told to me some thirty years later – with our Lily long since dead.

I can assure you from the experience of trying to get here, into the heart of all this over the past ten years, the dead do not easily give up the secrets they take with them into the grave and deeper still, to the bottomless seas of forgetfulness. But sometimes they leave a message that we may hear but not understand at the time, or we may be too wired into other biological urges, as I was at the age of fifteen. Lily's message, left in the heart of my grandmother in Liverpool, was delivered to me in Nanny's sunroom in Blackball as she was in full flight, summoning up her older sister. We must have been talking about the war: it came up all the time with Nanny, traumatised still by bombing in the Liverpool Blitz of May 1941. She spoke of an air-raid shelter in the garden; the poor dog going mental under the table as sirens howled their fiendish warnings in the night; of anti-aircraft guns booming and the terrifying explosions of bombs all around her, death coming nearer and nearer.

Lily had come back from Hamburg some years before this, for her niece Lillian's funeral in August 1934. Lillian, my mother's older sister, had been suffering from what was then an incurable condition, Hodgkin's lymphoma. She was nursed at home by my grandmother until the inevitable end. In her diary, on Monday the 13th of that month Nanny wrote, 'Lillian died, at 10.45 in my arms. My heart broke.' That same day, my mother was freed from the Bluecoat School nearby: 'Mr Wilson sent Polly home'. (Polly was Nanny's pet name for my mother, Mary.) The next entry is Friday the 17th: 'We buried Lillian, how beautiful she was, just asleep, & free from pain & trouble'. Nanny hardly had time to compose herself, in heartbreak. On Tuesday the 21st of August, we read, 'Mother had a stroke'. First her daughter; now her mother. By Saturday, she too is gone: 'Mother died at 9 a.m.'

Nanny was left alone to hold things together, to swallow her multiple griefs and manage these final farewells of her beloved family. Nanny's younger brother Hector arrives on the 27th; he stays at the Adelphi, but departs for Scotland the next day, leaving my Nanny to take care of the funeral. The following day, on Wednesday, 'We buried Mother'; on Thursday, when it is all over, 'Lillie came 5.30 am'. Too late. (This 'Lillie' is her sister, and our subject, Lily.) Writing this, having once again carefully taken down these bare, heartbroken details from the diary she left behind – that came to me when my own mother died in 2005 – it does not surprise me to read that a month later, Tuesday the 18th of September, she was 'taken ill with chill and nerves'. Nanny had suffered a perfectly understandable nervous breakdown.

What has this to do with Germany, then, and Hitler? Another death had preceded these departures: on the 2nd of August 1934, German President Paul von Hindenburg had died, and Adolf Hitler, already elected as chancellor and virtual dictator, announced that his office and that of president would be combined. In between Lillian's death and her grandmother's, Germans could vote in a plebiscite on the merging of the two offices and Hitler's new role as Führer. Some 95.7 percent of the population voted; 89.93 percent in favour of Hitler. Hindenburg's exit – the last link with Germany's pre-war imperial past – left no restraints at all now on Hitler: Führer and dictator, unhindered.

This seems to me the most likely moment at which Lily made the statement my grandmother never forgot, nor forgave, remembered perhaps in bitter hindsight in the light of what was to come, five years hence. 'Hitler,' Lily told her grieving sister, 'is a great man, Eunice. He is doing wonderful things for the German people.' I can still sense the bitterness and the anger in her retelling of this statement. Had events not unfolded as they did, had the war never happened, such a remark would have been forgotten; yet here Eunice was, thirty years later, pouring her anger and grief into her grandson.

That was August 1934; yet twenty years earlier, at the outbreak of the Great War; my great-aunt Lily, as the English wife of a German citizen, had found herself and their two children on enemy territory. How did she get there?

To answer this, we must go back to the late 1890s, a time when her father – my great-grandfather – had entered another of his manifestations: he was now a rubber-stamp maker, in Liverpool. Peter Daniel Bywater was a Welshman, born in rural Caersws in 1843. According to my grandmother, he had fled the area after assaulting a school master. Like thousands of other young Welshmen from all over the reach of the English throne, he had taken ship for America. His many adventures there, she said, included riding the short-lived Pony Express, meeting William Cody, and later fighting in the American Civil War. This latter claim I am able to verify from passenger records on one of his many later Atlantic crossings. His Civil War service was noted on the RMS *Ivernia*'s passenger manifest in 1909 as being that of a true US citizen.[2] 'Born USA', it reads – which we know was not the case. Was he claiming this, or was his grant of citizenship due to his wartime service? Whatever the truth, he could now travel as an American, and his children would certainly trade on this later in life.

Cody – as Buffalo Bill – certainly did come to Liverpool in 1891, with his Wild West Show. From my Nanny's account, she was thirteen at the time when her father took her – along with Lily and their brothers Ulysses and Hector – to the street parade of the performers, freshly landed from America.[3] Before his children's very eyes, their father, who had claimed he knew Cody well, strode out from the crowd as Cody rode by and called out, 'William!' Buffalo Bill called back, 'Peter!' Cody then leapt off his charger and, before the dumbstruck children, the two men embraced like the long-lost friends they were. From the eighty-year-old time zone where Nanny lived, these stories sounded authentic, invading our porous, pubescent worlds where anything could still be possible. Now, I have no doubt this is true. P.D. Bywater was quite a man, and by the time we meet him, later in life making his rubber stamps, he had more than filled his cup of life to the brim.[4]

It is as a rubber-stamp maker that our family's German connection begins. Needing supplies for his growing business, my great-grandfather made contact with Carl Hasenburg, a rubber trader from Hamburg. The city was at the time a centre for the growing trade of this increasingly important resource: in military terms alone, rubber was now a strategic material for the prosecution of colonial and imperial ambitions – and wars. Motor vehicles alone used rubber tyres in huge quantities, as well as engineering changes in seals and drive systems. Carl Hasenburg did indeed begin supplying P.D. Bywater with the necessary rubber.

In untangling family history, there are times we might wish we had never stumbled on certain things, while drawing blanks on other matters that we may have thought were important. There was my harmless old grandmother, Eunice – remembered by me now as spending many of her waking hours dozing in the sunroom after sewing, her life force seemingly drained. I would never have believed she was capable of faking her 1878 birthplace as New York when it was actually Liverpool.[5]

Opposite: Lilian Edith Bywater, London, around 1882. FAMILY ALBUM

The war was over. She was no longer employed in supervising other women in the shell factory at Quedgeley, now closed. She had played her part in making those deadly projectiles to be fired at German men, whose women, in similar munitions factories in Germany, were engaged in returning the favour. All of this time, Eunice had to suppress the ongoing heartache that her dear sister Lily was long since living in enemy territory in Hamburg, having in 1898 married that same Carl Hasenburg – a smooth salesman who had earlier fathered a boy child with Eunice, at a moment when rubber was sorely needed but evidently not to hand.

The detail, the chronology of these events is of course long lost and was never disclosed to me; it is revealed now only by simple mathematics. My dear mother, later in her life, told me that Nanny had been packed off to America by her parents to have Carl's child, hidden away with friends in New Jersey: the husband was, like her father, an old Civil War veteran. Whoever they were, these friends – I'm sure their images appear, unnamed, in the great family album Nanny kept with her always and bequeathed to my mother – they are now lost to time, as is that little German–Welsh boy, a nameless family-history ghost. I've never been able to establish a clear timeline, but from shipping records we know that 'Miss E.W. Bywater, age 27, sailed from New York to Liverpool, 31 January 1900, on the White Star Line vessel, *Oceanic*'. The age is wrong (she was twenty-two), but misspellings and mistakes are common enough on shipping manifests.

After Nanny's exile of shame, Carl had taken up where he left off, romancing her older sister Lily. What did the parental Bywaters think of this, a second German invasion of their gene pool? We'll never know, except that it did happen. Like thieves in the night, the Hasenburgs would slip away with their newborn son – Carl Hasenburg junior – and go to live in Hamburg, where Carl senior continued to ply his trade.

Eunice nurtured a lifelong mourning for her lost son in America, a grief she transferred on to this Carl, her nephew, the strange little German boy I would meet in her stories. She would sometimes sing to me a very strange song.

> There was a little woman as I've heard tell,
> She went to market her eggs for to sell.
> She went to market, all on a market day.
> And she fell asleep on the King's highway.
>
> By came a pedlar, his name it was Stout,
> And he cut her petticoats all round about.

When the poor woman awoke and realised what had happened, she began to weep under a darkening sky:

> 'Oh dearie, dearie me, this is none of I,
> Oh dearie, dearie me, this is none of I!'

Even as a restless and uncomprehending teenager, itching to be off and play war, this haunting got under my skin, sank into my soul. Nanny was mourning something lost; not even my adolescent distractions could ignore her. This may still have passed me by over time; there were so many stories filling the warm sunroom with its Singer sewing machine, her bedside cabinet covered in pillboxes, the ever-present bottles of Eau de Cologne No. 4711 she would apply, filling the air with the scents of another time and place. I would park myself on the closed lid of her commode, forgetful of its function, and listen to her stories.

In 1963, fifth form history saw to it I would not forget the song of the old woman and the pedlar. By then the old blaggard was transformed into a German trader, outfoxing his English counterpart in an 1896 Tenniel cartoon from *Punch* that appeared in our class history book, complete with the lines of the song that Nanny would sing to me.[6] Fifty years later, that cartoon, that song, recalled as I think of my Nanny's life – of her sister's husband who so badly used her – is telling me the truth. My grandmother is that woman, Carl Hasenburg is the pedlar, cutting her petticoats all round about.

TWO

Meeting the Remarkable Bywaters

ULYSSES, THE OLDER OF EUNICE'S TWO BROTHERS, HAD BY HIS early twenties made good use of his sojourn in Germany as a schoolboy, as well as his father's American experiences. By 1906 he was established in Dresden as Deputy Consul General for the United States. He revelled in the rich cultural life of the city: opera, museums, art galleries and a steady stream of well-to-do and attractive young women with their chaperones on the Grand Tour of Europe and, in many cases, husband hunting. Uly wrote to Hector, exhorting his younger brother with the naval obsession and a budding career as a journalist to come over and enjoy the good life of 'restaurants, cafes, beer gardens and pretty English girls'.[1] It wasn't long before Hector took the bait.

Hector's move to Dresden saw him enter a web of deceit, spun by his older, inventive sibling. In order to get his US passport renewed, Uly had faked their father's American citizenship and birth in Boston. This forgery enabled him to have his proof of birth waived. The document reads, 'Sixteen years American Consular official', signed for by

Opposite: Ulysses J. Bywater, 1902, before he moved to Dresden.
FAMILY ALBUM

a passport agent of the Department of State.[2] According to William Honan's biography, *Bywater: The Man Who Invented the Pacific War*, his job at the US Consulate was the third he had held 'based on the fiction', at a time when 'passports were then almost unknown and nationality was not a matter of serious concern'.[3] When Hector arrived in 1907, Uly informed him of the ruse and told his younger brother he would have to go along with it. Hector agreed and found a job as a journalist, in which he pursued his fascination with naval affairs in Germany. His ability with the German language and his access to bases on the North Sea informed his writings.

He was visited there by an Englishman who gave him a number to ring on his next trip to England. This proved to be a turning point. Hector made the trip to London, where he received a telephone call that directed him to 2 Whitehall Court. There, he was recruited as a spy by a man known only as 'C' – Sir Mansfield Smith-Cumming, chief of the Foreign Section of the Secret Service Bureau.

When his new boss was made aware of Hector Bywater's deception over his US nationality, in league with his brother, he urged Hector to have Uly certify him as an American citizen. With America as a likely neutral country in any future war with Germany, Hector could remain in the country as an American, while continuing to spy for Britain. Hector Charles Bywater, born in Tottenham, London in 1884, was now cleverly registered as Boston-born on 21 October 1881 – two years before compulsory registration of births was introduced in Massachusetts. Deception was becoming a family business.

By early 1909, Hector had married Emma Robinson in England and the couple had taken up residence in Dresden. Hector's life as a journalist and a spy and Uly's as an official in Dresden ran along parallel lines, until Uly left the US Consular Service in 1912 and began a career in banking. At one time we find that three of the British-born Bywater children were living in Germany: Lily and Carl were in Hamburg with their son Carl and their daughter Anita, born in Hamburg in 1910, and Uly and his Swiss wife Marguerite d'Arx were in Dresden. Between them the two brothers now had three German-born children. The odd one out, my Nanny Eunice, did not say if she had ever visited them; but her nephew, Carl junior, certainly came her way. What began to unfold was the trauma of blood relatives, divided by a war in which they would find themselves – as patriots and expatriates – at each other's throats. This family came to represent the madness of Europe in miniature: families at war, nations at war in a conflict that would destroy their comfortable worlds and irreversibly shape whatever history might lie before them.

By the outbreak of war, in the space of two years, my grandmother Eunice had been married and widowed. In July 1910, at the age of thirty-two, in Cheltenham, she met and married William Mitchell, a man six years her junior. Lillian, my aunt, was born the next year, in December, and William died the following October. Quite why my grandmother named her daughter after the sister who had, after all, married the man who had betrayed them both is one of those mysteries time has long foreclosed. War was threatening in the tinderbox of Europe. My Nanny's chances of finding another husband would be decided by a conflict soon to fell a generation of male suitors (although by 1918, none of the Bywaters or their spouses had fallen in this grim reaping). Hector, in the meantime, was back in England, having done his worst to ensure his brother-in-law Carl's native Germany was on the losing side. All this at a time when his sister Lily would endure, with her husband and son, the starvation years of the British naval blockade. Hector's espionage was meant to ensure German losses; in this form of total war, England's success meant he was attacking his own flesh and blood.

My grandmother, as we have seen, joined in the battle by working on the Home Front as a supervisor in a shell factory at Quedgeley, not far from her home in Cheltenham. These Munitionettes, as they were called in England, were themselves at risk. Chemical poisoning and explosions, as well as danger from the machinery itself, took many lives. It is hard to believe that my Nanny could ever have worked in such a place, in pursuit of an outcome that could, and almost certainly would, end the lives of some of her newfound German connections. Ernst Hasenburg (a possible relation of Carl, from the same tiny rural birthplace of Önkfeld, east of Düsseldorf) died at Passchendaele in

Hector (seated at table, left) and Emma (standing, centre), filling in for Ulysses at a US consular function, Dresden; note the three Native American guests. IMAGE COURTESY OF GLADYS E. BYWATER-CALNAN

August 1917. Could it have been a shell from Quedgeley that killed him? The apparent impersonality of war can disguise all manner of unlikely intimacies, except when seen up close and framed as here, in a family affair.

For my Nanny, the pull of America had still not weakened. After the work at the munitions factory ended, in August 1917 we find her applying for registration as a native citizen of the United States. In her application she states that she last left the United States in 1908, for England; she cites four different residences in Britain up until 1914.[4] I was taken completely by surprise to read here that her 'legal domicile' was in 'Wilkesbarre, Pa.' – her 'permanent residence'. She states that she desires 'to remain a permanent citizen of the United States', and that she most recently applied for registration in Liverpool 'on August 24, 1916'. As she is now a widow after the death of William Mitchell, she has resumed her citizenship by registering at the US Consulate in Liverpool. The Oath of Allegiance is solemnly sworn and signed, 'Eunice Winifred Mitchell' on 'this 28th day of August 1917'.

My Nanny, a naturalised American: is she a liar or, like her brothers, trading on her father P.D. Bywater's actual grant of honorary US citizenship for his service in the Civil War? We need to remember that passports, identification and proof of nationality were all a very different process in the early days of such important documents. Back then, it must have been far easier to get away with this. My instinct tells me this is simple: she was still searching for her adopted son. Perhaps she knew where he was, who he was with, and wanted to return there and be near him, even if she was unable to see him. Is that so hard to understand? Not for me.

Whatever was the truth of her purported 'legal domicile' in Wilkes-Barre, Pennsylvania, Nanny would never go back to America. Soon after the war's end, she met Samuel Thomas Woollam, the man who became my mother's father – the grandfather I never knew, only ever met as another lost beloved in my mother's stories.

What, then, had become of her brother Hector? At the outbreak of war, by this time a covert lieutenant commander in the Royal Navy, he was back in England on leave. It was too dangerous for him to return to Germany: he was now on transfer to Naval Intelligence. In the autumn of 1915 he was sent on a mission to New York, to infiltrate a German spy ring that was planting bombs in the coal bunkers of ships bound for Britain. The spies had managed to sink over forty vessels in this manner before the ring was broken, due in part to Hector's success. Hector's secret war work (no uniform and, later, no pension and no honours) would leave him disillusioned in the peace when it came, and he returned to his journalist's trade.[5] With Uly's help, he had renewed his US passport in October 1915, as part of the Admiralty's conviction that retaining his false American citizenship would be an advantage. On his return from this highly dangerous work in New York, he then had to be registered in Britain as an alien.

Ulysses had by now obtained work as a banker in Milan, working for the National City Bank of New York. He, too, was applying for re-registration as an American citizen. He had left Dresden in 1912

and gone to Rome, where he worked in the US Consulate until 1916. When Uly swore the Oath of Allegiance on 15 March 1917, he was carrying on a now established Bywater tradition of duplicity. Postwar, this trait would backfire on Hector: trying to re-establish his British nationality, he got into a stoush with MI5 and the Home Office. He did manage to make his case and prove his British birth, thus regaining his citizenship, but the tortuous process was a bitter one for a man who had risked his life for England. He needed this in 1926 for the sake of his Dresden-born son Robin, who was turning sixteen in England and wanted to claim British nationality for himself, at a time when German citizens were still unwelcome.

Eunice, meanwhile, as mentioned, had remarried in 1919 to Samuel Thomas Woollam, a dairyman from Cheltenham who was recently widowed. The couple set sail for New Zealand from Southampton on the SS *Remuera* on 3 March 1921, with my aunt Lillian – Eunice's daughter from her first marriage. Samuel was a Salvationist, on a return mission to the country he had lived in before the war, dairy farming at Parewanui near Bulls with his first wife, Annie Maria Pendell, from 1911 to 1914. My Nanny, pregnant on this voyage, gave birth to my mother in Castlecliff, Whanganui, on 10 November 1921 – beginning the New Zealand family line. By 1926, however, they were back in Liverpool as my grandfather Samuel had suffered, while in New Zealand, the first of a series of strokes that would eventually kill him. The journey south had not been kind to them; and the world was soon in the grip of the Great Depression, coming hard on the heels of the 1929 stock market crash.

Nanny's sister, my great-aunt Lily, had survived the war in Hamburg but was left in a broken and defeated Germany where the deep wounds of war, simmering below the surface, broke out in violent assassinations on the same streets where crippled war veterans begged for charity. Many former military men – those who had never

Opposite: Eunice Winifred Mitchell (née Bywater), munitions worker, Quedgeley, Gloucestershire, 1916–18. FAMILY ALBUM

A war-weary Hector Bywater, June 1919, at 23 Whitmore Road, Bromley.
FAMILY ALBUM

accepted their defeat on the battlefield, blaming instead betrayals by socialists and Jews in positions of political influence – were biding their time, waiting for Germany to rise again. One of those so disaffected happened to be an Austrian – Adolf Hitler, a former soldier, now a failed art student with a talent for rabble-rousing and a thirst for revenge.

In this unstable new age, the creative spirits of the Weimar Republic burst forth in a remarkable wave of artistic productions that would help to define modernity, even as the political culture that permitted their rise staggered and finally fell, sabotaged by a festering resentment of defeat that the Nazis would own – and weaponise. By 1933 that same sociopathic drifter, Hitler, would steer his thugs and schemers into the Reichstag. They would unleash a dominion far darker than anything

Hitler is greeted by the masses as he is driven through the crowd, Germany, c.1936. (From *Germany: The Olympic Year*, Volk und Reich Verlag, Berlin, 1936.) HERITAGE IMAGE PARTNERSHIP LTD/ALAMY STOCK PHOTO

Europe had endured in the previous war, the same 'stab in the back' this dictator and his streetfighters regarded as unfinished business.

The few scraps of this story that my Nanny passed on to me of her sister's part in this drama set me off in search of Lily and her husband, Carl. Finally it drew me to Germany – picking up whatever traces remained of their lives in the written record, learning German, finding a source of finance to get me there, applying for residencies and funding, making contacts, chancing my arm and seeing what doors might open. History is never boring: it never truly dies but hides in the darkest places and dares us to come looking. In every crowd, in every picture we see of lost times and forgotten humans, there is always a witness; always there is an individual, a relative, a stranger looking back at us viewers, asking a question that can feel like this: 'Were you here with me, where would you stand, what would you do, if you knew in your heart of hearts that you could not agree with this mob?'

It goes to prove how dangerous an occupation it is to embark on a family history. One wonders about the masochism inherent in the modern hordes of genealogists who, like me, set out to uncover honour and greatness, perhaps; more often than not, coming up for air with proof of their opposites: cruelty, selfishness, all of life's shadows. Genealogy is dangerous: our dead, buried like countless unexploded shells lying, waiting, in the fields of France and Belgium, rusting away, exploding when some careless plough, in the oncoming years, strikes munitions fired long ago.

From my Nanny's stories, I had a string of connections to her sister Lily and to her nephew Carl, but little concrete evidence. That was all to change midway through 1990, when I was working in a bookshop in Maidstone, Kent. My wife and I had moved to England with our young family in 1987, where I got a job in a care home in rural Kent. Feeling burnt out after eighteen months of live-in pressure, housed in a therapeutic community that belied its vision, I'd changed roles and moved into town. There I became a bookseller, a job that suited my literary ambitions, working in a newly opened quality bookshop – Waterstones. As well as selling books, I was back to reading them; it felt like I was recovering from a kind of starvation. I'd started writing again – a calling that had been stifled and swamped by years of ecclesiastical service and community-building back in New Zealand. I was back where I belonged, a move triggered by an obituary for the American poet and short-story writer Raymond Carver, who died in August 1988. Reading of his life's journey, his addictions, which were also mine, I knew it was time to write – or die within.

On lunchbreak at the shop, idly skimming a publisher's new title material, I opened a catalogue to be confronted by a cover image that literally shouted, *'BYWATER'* – *The Man Who Invented the Pacific War*. I choked on my sandwich. Uncle Hector, my goodness! Here he was: in fact, a whole book devoted to his life and influence, written by a seasoned American journalist, 'Chief Cultural Correspondent for the New York Times', no less – one William H. Honan. The excitement of this random discovery returns, even now. Here at last was an external warrant to my Nanny's stories, already given their attestation in our growing years by the collection of Hector's books she had with her. There were hundreds of ship's postcards we rifled through on wet days in Blackball – images of naval vessels, all shapes and sizes from the late nineteenth century onwards, collected by her precocious younger brother and bequeathed to her on his death.

The next time a publisher's representative for Macdonald & Company arrived at the bookshop, I buttonholed the poor man in my excitement: I was related to the subject of this book! Could I get a copy? Certainly, a gratis volume would be sent to me. Did he have any information on the writer? Yes indeed, he would make sure I was sent Bill Honan's contact details with the book. All of these promises he faithfully carried out. I still have that same copy, signed indeed by the author on the 15th of September 1990, and signed as well, a little later in the year, by Hector's son Robin (also known as Hector, the Reverend H.W.R. Bywater). Of this delightful reverend gentleman, more later ... But first, to my meeting Bill Honan.

I wrote to Bill Honan at the address supplied, telling him who I was, and my delight at discovering his book. I told him that my grandmother Eunice was Hector's older sister; that we'd always known about him, but now, with this book, there was the proof of his genius. Bill replied that he was delighted to hear of this. He told me he was due to come over for the UK launch of *Bywater*, which was set to take place on 15 September 1990, Battle of Britain Day, the fiftieth anniversary of the Battle of Britain. He would love to meet me in London and show me around some of Hector's haunts – which he did. With his long-suffering family in tow, Bill took us on a grand tour of these haunts, including the building at no. 2 Whitehall (now the Royal Horseguards Hotel) where, as we have seen, my great-uncle was recruited into British Naval Intelligence in 1908. He went on to spy for his country thereafter, especially in the war of 1914–18, and lived on to write many great tales of his exploits and close shaves.[6]

Better still, Bill Honan gave me contact details for Hector's son Robin (and for others of the Bywater whānau he had interviewed

> For Jeffrey Holman, a delightful companion and part of a fabulous family, who will now continue this story where I have left off.
> Warmly,
> Bill Honan
> 9/15/90
>
> Hector W. R. Bywater
> (Son of Hector a.k.a. "Robin")

Bill Honan's signature in his book *Bywater*, signed a little later that same year by Hector Bywater's son Robin.

for the book). Robin was someone who knew my grandmother – his aunt – and had met his cousin Lillian in 1934, shortly before she died. At last, someone living, who was prepared to speak to me about his relationships with, and knowledge of, the Bywater clan – especially Great-aunt Lily. I wrote to him from Maidstone, at the address provided by Bill Honan: 15 Bath Road, Mickleover, Derby. He was prompt in responding; a tiny blue envelope arrived in August, containing a likewise tiny sheet of paper covered in a spidery hand which, as I deciphered and read, made me almost shout for joy. Here was a living, breathing Bywater: my Nanny's nephew, stepping out of her history, with stories that had sunk into my depths thirty years gone, now coming back to life. I must have arrived into his old age as something of a bolt from the blue.

2: Meeting the Remarkable Bywaters

Bill Honan, London, September 1990, with his biography of Hector.

Dear Mr Holman,
Many thanks for your letter which is a pleasant surprise, as I lost touch with the rest of the Bywater clan after Uncle Uly's death,[7] although many years afterwards I made contact with his son John, who was American consul in Geneva. He and his wife visited us on several occasions, and since his death some years ago, his widow, Gladys Bywater-Calnan has kept in touch, and has helped Mr Honan with photos etc, for the biography.

He wrote that he had retired from his position as an Anglican priest at St Alkmunds parish church. 'My sister and I have been very thrilled to see the book [*Bywater*] published at last,' he continued – as Bill Honan's years of research had left them both wondering if they would

Lilian Edith (Lily) Hasenburg, passport photo, 1934.
ANCESTRY.COM, PUBLIC DOMAIN

survive to see it. He was still mourning 'the death of my dear wife in January'; and now, of course, there was his own failing health, crippled as he was with arthritis. But there was more:

> Needless to say, I will be very pleased to meet and talk with you, and hear what happened to my Dad's sister Aunt Lily Hassenberg and her son Karl after World War II, as I know her Jewish husband was murdered by the Nazis.

This was quite a shock to me: at this early point in my quest, I knew nothing of Aunt Lily's marriage to Carl Hasenburg, nor of his heritage: I was to glean this information much later, in 2014. In fact, prior to this, I had no inkling that Aunt Lily was touched in any way by the Holocaust. The Reverend Bywater wrote more:

I know Uncle Uly managed to get her out of Germany through the Red Cross and she was interned on the Isle of Man, but I never heard what happened to her afterwards.

He was correct on his aunt's internment: he could only have got this information from his uncle, Lily's brother. I assumed back then that it was from Uly he learned about the murder of Lily's Jewish husband.

Later research has since shown that Uly was indeed in Germany in 1940, before the launch of Hitler's May Blitzkrieg. He had travelled there on his fake US citizenship, as a journalist for the newspaper *Paris-soir* (his multilingualism, spoken of by my Nanny, had served him well).[8] Uly does mention in his first newspaper report that he was visiting a relative (that would have been Lily). Here was something that my grandmother had never mentioned: not to me, and not to my mother, as Mum knew nothing of her Aunt Lily having a Jewish husband. We know Lily was singing Hitler's praises to Nanny in 1934; yet she must have seen instances of Nazi anti-Semitism by that stage, as it was also widely reported in the British press. Who was this mysterious Jewish husband?

To the best of my knowledge back then, the Reverend Bywater had all the other details correct. He also mentioned he had a copy of Bill Honan's book about his father, waiting for me to see when I came. He ended with some details of my family: 'When I was in Liverpool, I met Lillian [my aunt], who died soon after, but I never met cousin Mary [my mother] and was unable to attend her wedding [in London in 1943]'.

I booked a ticket and two days later travelled to see Robin at his home in Derby, packing my newly acquired Aiwa Walkman cassette recorder. Some edited transcripts of our conversation follow in the next chapter, where Robin spills his heart to me, this godwit from the south.

THREE

Cousin Robin and the Jewish Husband

THE TRAIN JOURNEY FROM LONDON TO DERBY AND THE TAXI ride to Robin Bywater's humble brick home in Mickleover, a quiet suburb, gave no indication of the depths of twentieth-century history quietly fading away in the person of my newfound relative, so willing to bring the past back to life for anyone who would listen. It wasn't long before my eighty-year-old repository of these depths would unwind. We sat in his sunny lounge with my Walkman running. He showed me Bill Honan's book, and original copies of his father Hector's books: *The Great Pacific War* and *Their Secret Purposes: Dramas and Mysteries of the Naval War*.[1] It all felt very strange: sitting with my first cousin once removed, the son of my great-uncle, my grandmother's nephew. It was then twenty-five years since her death in 1967, days when she had spoken of Hector, Ulysses and Lily as if they too, were in the room. It was hard not to feel that they were.

Robin needed no encouragement: as the tape rolled, he unfolded details from the shadows my grandmother's outline had given me. Emma, his mother, 'knew Auntie Lily in Dresden ... she married a German Jew ... he was Jewish'. This was the beginning of my belief that Lily had been caught up in the fate of those Gentiles who had

3: Cousin Robin and the Jewish Husband

Reverend Robin Bywater at his home in Derby, September 1990.

chosen Jewish partners. Surely, if she had known this, my grandmother would have told me? Robin said that during the Great War, 'they were in a very difficult position, because [Lily] was of British origin, married to a German'. I'm absorbed by this revelation, and by his claim that in the Second World War, 'her husband was rounded up by the Nazis and either killed, or sent to a camp. After [he] was taken by the Nazis, before the US came into the war, Uly went over [to Germany] with the American Red Cross' – and he was instrumental in getting Lily out of Germany, to England. We now know that Lily did indeed get to England.[2] Robin is correct when he says, 'she was put in an internment camp on the Isle of Man ... and I lost all connection'. He speaks of his mother Emma's gratitude to Aunt Lily, when his father Hector had been working at the US Consulate in Dresden before the Great War: '[Lily] was very kind and helped her a lot ... a stranger in a strange land. Many years later, my mother said [to me],

"If you can do anything to help Aunt Lily, do so" – but I could not do anything, I did not know if she was in England, or Germany [after the Second World War] ... or what happened to her son, Carl [Pip]'.

There was more enlightenment – and some confusion – to come, when the issue of Lily's son Carl came up in the conversation. Robin said, 'What happened to Pip? I don't know, I don't think anybody knows. Cousin John [Bywater, Uly's son], who died three or four years ago, even he didn't know what had happened to him, whether he stayed on in Germany when his mother came to England, or he ended up in the Eastern Front or something ...'.

It is obvious to me now that, in 1990, Robin had no idea his cousin Carl and German wife Irma had been living in England, mostly in London, since 1924 – a three-hour journey by train from his house in Derby. Nor did he know that Carl had died three years earlier, in 1987; and Irma had died a year later, in 1988. Robin's father Hector and his mother Emma certainly knew Carl and Irma were living in London, as my grandmother's 1934 diary entry will later reveal. How could Robin not have known? My Nanny Eunice records her meeting with Irma on the second of October 1934, and with her nephew Pip (Carl), Irma's husband, three days later, on the fifth.[3] Robin does not seem to know of these later family contacts with his cousin Carl. Has he forgotten – especially as he was well aware of his cousin Lillian's death, which brought the family members together at that time? On all the other details, though, he seems very sharp indeed.

The fact that he refers to Carl as Pip (as did my grandmother) is hardly a reason to suggest that he knew of his cousin only through his pet name, in their childhood years. It seems highly unlikely that after meeting Aunt Lily – Carl's mother – in Dresden before the Great War, and during the conflict, he would not have been aware of his cousin's move to England. He never mentions this later history. The tape later revealed some breaks in Robin's contact with his other family members, such as his cousin John. He was aware John had been in the diplomatic service, so he contacted the US Consulate in London. Documents revealed John Bywater as US consul in Geneva, at some time in the 1950s. Robin tried to get in touch, but 'heard nothing for ten years'. It was not until the death of John's father, Uly, in 1961 that contact with his cousin was re-established: 'They [John and his wife Gladys] visited us several times in Derby.' I wondered, transcribing this recording later, did John Bywater also tell Robin the Nazi–Jewish story about Aunt Lily? There is no way of knowing now, but Robin claims he got it from Uly. His uncle would have known. Why invent this? Did Lily and Carl split up at some time, and had she remarried, to someone of Jewish ancestry? Only my great-uncle Uly knows the truth – and he is gone.

The focus of this quest shifts now, from my stalled search in 1990 when, for any number of reasons, including a short four-month rebound to New Zealand soon after this encounter, I lost contact with Robin. I came back to the UK, then moved from Maidstone to London in early 1991, followed by another spell as a bookseller at Waterstones, Charing Cross Road. I somehow lost the impetus to follow through on the search for Carl Hasenburg and my other Bywater relations. The work lay dormant as I got on with surviving daily journeys to work by cycle, bus and Tube; writing poetry, more and more, enrolling in wonderful adult education classes in creative writing at City Lit in Central London. In 1997 came my serious return home: I went back to university to finish a BA degree, abandoned in the mid 1970s.

Ten years on, with my one-time unfinished academic life from way back reprised and fulfilled, I hear Germany calling. I see the shadow of Lily's life falling across my path. I'm somehow restless – or is it Lily's ghost who is restless?

FOUR

Nanny's Address Book and Mormon Helpers

> Tell me my friends
> What journey ever ends
> Where the heart intends?
> — A.R.D. FAIRBURN[1]

WHEN I STARTED ON HIS TRAIL, IT WAS CLEAR THAT CARL Hasenburg senior would not be easy to find. All I had was a family story that he had fathered a child with my grandmother Eunice, either before or after he married her older sister, Lily. Eunice was sent to America to have the baby – a boy – and left him behind in a heartbreaking adoption. That was all: no proof; no mother of mine, since her death in 2005, to check my recall of her mother's story; no other source but this. Of his family – my great-aunt Lily and her son Pip – there were other tales my Nanny told. I knew she hosted her nephew for English holidays, a surrogate for her lost son; that in the 1930s, as the Nazis rose to power, her sister had visited and had spoken of her admiration for Hitler. There did exist a few precious resources: Eunice's family photo album, her address book, and Aunt Lillian's 1934 diary – the year she died – taken over by her grieving mother, who recorded some significant traces.

Another resource was the Ancestry.com website, something I had resisted joining as a paid subscriber. Now that I was beginning to dig deeper, it was obvious I'd have to give in and pay the price the Mormons were asking. Yes, the Mormons. The website was launched by them in 2006, quickly gobbling up the births, deaths and marriages databases we were once able to search gratis. Theirs is a huge database, on file from years of searching worldwide, collecting the details of dead relatives, that they might be baptised for them, post-mortem, so to speak. This is based on a single verse in the Apostle Paul's first letter to the church in Corinth, writing to its members of this practice (1 Corinthians 15:29).[2] The Latter-day Saints in Utah lifted this passage from his teaching on the resurrection of the dead, making it their very serious business to get all departed loved ones right with the Lord.

Now it was my turn to be involved, in a kind of resurrection of the dead to literary life on earth. The Mormons proved to be indispensable helpers, along with Findmypast.co.uk and other websites, such as vitalcertificates.co.uk. This last company will find a copy of birth, death and marriage (BDM) certificates and other material and send a scan within ten days – for a price. I've been able to find birth and death dates, ship's passages, census information and electoral roll addresses, and from this wide net, a picture of Carl Hasenburg emerges from the sea of forgetfulness. The 1901 UK census shows that Carl and my great-aunt Lily, along with their one-year-old son Carl Ulysses (Pip), were residing in Birkenhead, England, where they had married in 1898. His profession was given as a 'Sub-Manager India Rubber Trade', and his nationality was recorded as German. The Hasenburgs then seem to disappear from UK records. I got lucky, however: I stumbled online upon the death of one Carl Ulysses Hasenburg in Westminster in July 1987 – and the whole axis of the story begins to shift. I'd always imagined that Carl and Lily's children – my Nanny's 'Pip' and his sister Anita – had lived and died in Germany. But this is him.

Robin had told me that Lily had escaped from Germany during the war, after the Nazis murdered her Jewish husband. Yet Nanny had never mentioned this background; nor the fact that my great-uncle Ulysses had been involved, with the Red Cross, in helping their sister escape to England. Nor had my grandmother ever mentioned that Lily was then interned on the Isle of Man as, being married to a German, she was the wife of an enemy alien. What a family, what a story – and what was there to come?

At this point in the search, my mother's sister Lillian's diary and my Nanny's address book were recovered. They'd been packed away during renovations, before the onset of the Christchurch earthquakes from 2010 onwards, and left undisturbed for five years. With good reason to pay closer attention, in 2015 I began to explore them in detail.

The letter 'H' in the address book was a goldmine: it recorded all the places Aunt Lily and her husband and family had lived in Hamburg, updated as they moved around the city. This was exciting; but a later entry in my grandmother's hand (in biro rather than her original ink fountain pen) was much more intriguing: '"Pip", C Hasenburg, 1 Palace Court, Bayswater, London'. It slowly dawned on me that Pip, the character in Nanny's stories from my childhood, was also named Carl. It was obvious he was then living in London, but how long had he been there? There were more discoveries as I annotated the entries my grandmother had made in Lillian's 1934 diary. As well as the heartbreaking cries of grief my Nanny recorded, as Lillian sickened and died, there were notes of visits and visitors: family, and friends she had seen, all of those who had come to visit her, before and after the funeral. In early October she had gone to London to stay with her brother Hector and his second wife, Francesca; on Friday the fifth, she wrote: 'met Evelyn and then on to Pip and Billy[?] – very nice evening'. Now it was clear to me that by 1934 at least, Carl Ulysses was back in London. And there were more realisations to come. It was like entering a dark place, growing accustomed to the change, seeing strange faces.

As I look at this entry in the diary, what strikes me is that the little boy she spoke of to me, back in Blackball, was never referred to as the mature man she visited on that day – when he would have

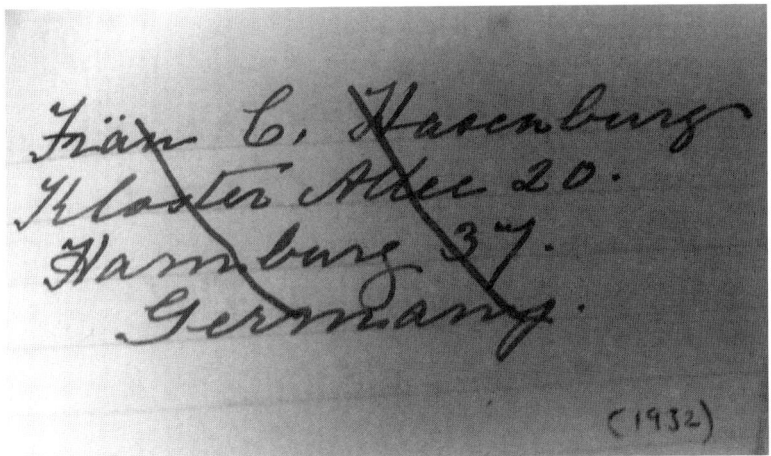

My grandmother's address book, with Lily's address in Hamburg.

been around forty-five years old. The fact that the address entry is written in blue ballpoint is significant; all the addresses written in ballpoint, rather than fountain pen, date from after my Nanny's arrival in New Zealand in 1951 to live with my family. The London address should have alerted me to something I finally worked out a few weeks later: my Nanny was still in contact with him after her arrival here, and very likely up until her death in 1967 (when she was in her late eighties, and he was in his sixties). The cheeky German-speaking boy, little Carl, 'Pip', would morph into Charles before my eyes: I pictured him, a retired security officer – as noted by his next of kin, his wife Irma, on the copy of his death registration in June 1987.

It was all there in the copy I had ordered from Vital Certificates. My motive for obtaining this was to find the name of the informant. There she was, Irma Hertha Hasenburg, his widow, present at his death from bronchopneumonia and carcinoma of the bladder. My guess was he had married her in Germany and, at some time before 1934, they had moved back to England. If his father was Jewish, did this have any bearing on his return? Carl was a British subject from his birth in Liverpool and could rightfully go back to

England and reside. Why would he? Until his twenties, his life was that of an English-born German boy residing in Germany. Here was a new name for the developing family tree: I added Irma and Charles Hasenburg to my searches. This brought up a fresh catch online: according to immigration records in Belgium, young Carl had passed through Antwerp on his way to Germany with his parents, sometime after 1901 and before 1915. That placed them back in Germany before the war broke out. The Belgian transcript gave his father's birth year as 1874 in the town of Önkfeld, near Cologne. More and more stitches were appearing in the weaving of this tapestry.

Further searches discovered a Hasenburg living in Radevormwald near Önkfeld in 1901: 'Hasenburg, Emil, Schmeid' at Grünenbaum Hof, an estate with seventy inhabitants. Emil was a blacksmith (Schmeid) and very possibly a relative of Carl's. In the same search, a reference to Carl Hasenburg in the *London Gazette* of 11 April 1922 threw up a long list of German names; this proved to be a 'list of Former Alien Enemies Landed from March 1–31'. They had been listed as required under the Aliens Restriction Act 1919 and the Registration Act of 1920, an update of the 1914 wartime regulations that extended the powers to impose restrictions on aliens. Aliens were obliged to register with the police; they were subject to deportation and were restricted as to where they could live. They were barred from jobs such as those in the Civil Service, and suffered other harassments, in order to protect the jobs of 'indigenous white Britons'. Was it Carl senior or junior, caught in this net? A family visit by the father, or a move back to Britain by the son, with his German wife? We were getting warm.

There were numerous local body rolls in London that placed Charles (Carl) and Irma Hasenburg at a variety of addresses from 1931 through to 1964, including at 1 Palace Court, Bayswater, for the year 1951 – the address that appears in my grandmother's address book, once she is in New Zealand. As often happens when the trail heats up, the name 'Irma' seemed somehow familiar. It occurred to me that when I had transcribed the entries from my aunt Lillian's diary, I had seen that name before.

4: Nanny's Address Book and Mormon Helpers

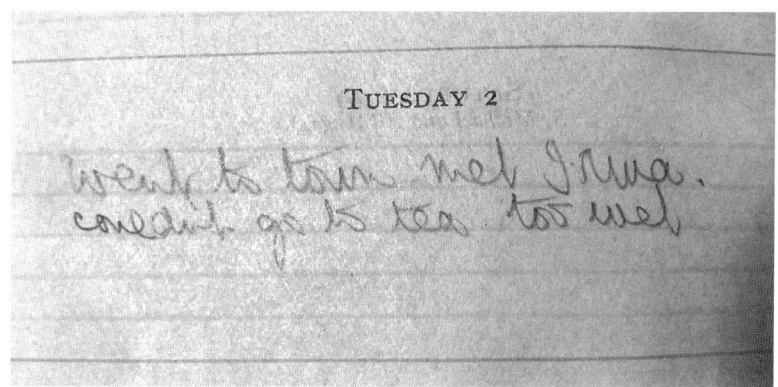

Nanny's diary entry, when she 'met Irma', 2 October 1934.

A quick check revealed that on Tuesday 2 October 1934, my grandmother had written, 'Went to town met Irma, couldn't go to tea, too wet'. This meant she had met Pip's wife and had visited them in London – very likely quite often – yet in all the many family stories she told me, this was never mentioned. Was she fixated on the boy?

What intrigues me is that, of the seven local body rolls sourced online, there are none for the years 1939–45; we can only assume they were not kept by local councils during the war years. Despite the younger Carl having lived in England at least since the 1930s (and possibly since 1922), were they interned in the war years, as was his mother Lily, simply because of their German name and connections? Irma was German-born, after all, and suspicion of all such nationals was rampant. Thousands of innocent Germans, many of them Jewish refugees, were swept up in this net from 1940 onwards.[3]

I had begun to think I might not find anything else about Carl senior. But when I got to Germany later in the year and was digging into German archives, his name came up in a search of directories. After pages of fruitless trolling through military records, street addresses and telephone numbers, I came on the last page to a list of Hamburg businesses in 1928 – and there he was. I had to look twice – there are plenty of Hazenbergs and Karls out there – but something about the address looked familiar. I remembered my Nanny's address book and a list of her sister Lily's Hamburg residences, and there she was, 'Frau C. Hasenburg, Kloster Allee 20, Hamburg 37, Germany' – the same address as in the directory on the screen in front of me. Bullseye! At last, I had an actual address – and now there was something concrete on which I could start to build the search.

Not only did I have an address in Germany, now I had a time and a place. The photograph of Carl in the album, taken in Hamburg years earlier, stared back at me from the wall above the desk where I'd placed it weeks ago. He seemed more alive than ever. What appeared to be the name of a company at this address was intriguing: 'Rohgummi u. Chemik'. Was this the firm he was working for? I searched the name and found a German translation that explained the mystery: Rohgummi is raw rubber. It took me back to his meeting with my family in Liverpool and his marriage to my great-aunt in 1898. Carl was still in the rubber business. I wondered if he had stayed involved with my great-grandfather and his rubber-stamp manufacturing right up until the old man's death in March of the previous year, 1927. The blank square of my German jigsaw was now beginning to reveal tiny but interconnected pieces, and it was taking a human shape. I was also about to discover the danger of rabbit holes.

The next step was to send for Irma's death certificate and find out who the informant was – perhaps they did have a child after all? When the copy arrived ten days later, it seemed that this was not the case. Irma Hertha Hasenburg, born in Germany on the sixth of June 1901, had died in Westminster Hospital on the first of December 1988, a year after her husband. The informant was one Dumiso Ncube, listed under his qualification to identify the dead woman as 'occupier'. Her usual address was on Bishops Bridge Road, London W2, and I assumed he was now living there. Searches of his name revealed a man now living in Yeovilton as a manager in the NHS. His profile

Opposite: Carl Hasenburg, Hamburg, 1919; from my grandmother's album.
FAMILY ALBUM

on the LinkedIn website had him a postgraduate medical student at the Polytechnic of Central London in the year Irma died. Was he a boarder with the Hasenburgs? As retirees with no children, perhaps they needed extra income.

A message to him yielded no response – which can simply mean wait, try again, or look elsewhere. Another search revealed that Irma's estate had remained unclaimed, and that enquiries from relatives or informants were welcome. My hopes were dashed when another link revealed her case had been 'resolved' in 2011: this meant that somebody else out there was either related or interested. Could we find them? More random facts emerged in another search for Carl junior: it seems he was a kind of inventor. In 1931 he was listed as one of three people registering a patent on an improved bracket for an electric lamp. He was living at 69 Portsdown Road, Maida Hill, in March 1930, when the application was made. Here at least was proof of his residence in London, two years after his parents were known to be living and working in Hamburg. It was like picking my way half-blind through a maze, every now and then finding a string with the label, 'Try Me'. The trick seemed to be to expect nothing and try anything.

Hot and cold, hot, and cold. I had contacted Lily's great-nephew, Clive Newland, through a fortuitous series of events. I was beginning to think my letter to him might have landed on an old address, when the post revealed his reply was from Chesham, in Buckinghamshire. He was very happy to have heard from me and enjoyed reading my letter. He is the youngest of Hector's grandchildren but knew little of the Bywater side of the family, as Emma (his grandmother) had died when he was young. On the plus side, he was very keen for us to meet and made me an open invitation to come and stay for a few days.

Clive said he had forwarded a copy of my letter to his two older brothers, Martin and Nicholas. A week later, an email arrived from Martin, now living between summer in Ontario and winter in Florida. Seven years older than Clive, he remembered his grandmother Emma Bywater 'well into the sixties'. He knew for instance 'that Hector travelled to Germany and Europe in the twenties and thirties as there were postcards and stamps that were passed down when my grandmother died'. He believed these trips were related to his work 'as a naval correspondent, reporting to the British government on the state of the German navy'. He felt that on his travels, Hector may well have visited his sister Lily. He had no recall of his mother, Sylvia, saying she had an aunt, let alone one who had once lived in Germany.

The mention of those postcards excited me: my grandmother had a wad of postcards, sent by her peripatetic younger brother Hector, that featured photographs of warships of the world's navies. As boys, my brother and I would shuffle through the cards with their images of mighty dreadnoughts, unaware of what lay behind them. Perhaps these newfound relatives might have clues as to where Lily and Carl were during Hitler's rise to power? I got to work, sending them images of their mother and the Bywater family they might never have seen, harvested from the treasure chest of Nanny's family album.

Serendipity shook hands with the surreal: I felt once more that the story was as much in the process, the search, as in any result, if there were to be one. Writing memoir and history, we are prey to something novelists need not consider: the inadvisability of stepping away from known facts, into wishful thought. We may get things wrong, may speculate, but we should never invent or embellish. We may be in search of the dead, but it is the living discovered along the way who will prove just as interesting – often just as eccentric, and at times, just as uncooperative.

My search for Irma Hasenburg's death certificate informant, Dumiso Ncube, hung over me. I'd had no response from my message to him on LinkedIn, so pursued him further via a message to the NHS trust in Yeovilton, where he was listed as last being employed. A kindly administrator responded to my enquiry with the news that 'Mr Ncube no longer works for the Trust', but she would send my message on to him. A few days later, an email came: 'Dear Mr Holman, Unfortunately I do not recall your relative or being an informant for her passing. I note that in an email to one of my former employers you have suggested that she spoke to me. I am afraid I did not know her, and I am sorry I am unable to help you and the rest of your family'. Now, another dead end – how many Dumiso Ncubes could there be?

I paid to join a site called People Tracer, and discovered there was a Dumiso Joe Ncube living in Altrincham, south of Manchester. Should I try him next, or was I just barking up one too many wrong trees? Namespedia.com estimated there are over 700 Ncubes living in Britain, more than anywhere else in the world (there also seemed to be many in Zimbabwe). Surely someone, somewhere out there, knows something about Carl and Irma Hasenburg and has what I am looking for – some news about my great-aunt and her German husband? A Facebook chat with a Zimbabwean writer friend, Chris Mlalazi, revealed that Ncube was indeed a local name: 'It is Ndebele, which is my tribe, but our people are scattered all over, especially in South Africa'.

The answer would come much later, thanks to my wife's sharp editorial eye during later edits. I now know that *occupier*, on the death certificate, had nothing at all to do with Irma Hasenburg's home; the term occupier referred to a medical official from the institution reporting the death. Red-faced, I sigh: it's never too late to learn. Wild goose chases and dead ends are bread and butter in this kind of adventure. I keep believing that persistence wins results; there is always more to each family story, waiting for us to come and stand before forgotten graves and mossy plaques.

The search for Lily seems to have gone cold. I am a long way from any information about her life, stories that might reward me with human details. Did Lily go back to Germany after 1948? That's possible. If not, she must have died in England, perhaps even having changed her German married name back to Bywater? This seems unlikely, and more searches don't appear to support this. I sense she is in England somewhere and so is more of her story, in those years between 1943 and 1948 where the evidence, so far, is missing. Her history challenges me to come closer: 'I am the Past, but who are you?'

It's time to change countries. I've always known that to get any kind of clarity I would have to go to Germany, to find out more about Carl's background and his married life with my great-aunt, after the turn of the century and on into the Second World War. I need to make the move.

An application for a writing residency in Berlin 2013–14 misses out. I try a second possibility: a scholarship with the Goethe-Institut in Germany. I write to their office in Wellington, detailing my plans. A friendly reply advises me that they have no funds available to support a writing project like mine, but why not apply to them for an eight-week German language course scholarship? I do just that and somehow, wonderfully, it is granted. I am to go to Freiburg in February and March of 2014 and stay on an extra month to do some research. This all seems fine – until it turns out that we will be having earthquake repairs made to our house in April 2014. It is not a good idea for me to be away when that is happening, leaving my wife Jeanette on her own for three months, after we've already had to move out into a temporary home, and then back to our repaired house, several weeks later. I let Goethe know about this – *Aber, alles ist gut!* I can choose a date later in the year, and this time it will be in Berlin, from 27 October to 18 December. Berlin! *Fantastisch! Toll!*

In the meantime, I enrol in Hagley Community College evening classes: a Beginners Deutsch course on Wednesday nights with Norma Orlowski. This proves to be very helpful: the pace is slow, the classes are well run, and Norma is an excellent teacher. Making a start is what matters. New Year 2014 rolls around as I continue with the search, then in April–May everything is paused as our house is emptied for those earthquake repairs. Packing every knife, fork and spoon, the entire household into storage in the garage, then relocating around the corner, five weeks of temporary rental accommodation; moving back in again to our repainted and replastered rooms, three years after the first shocks – it all took a bit out of me. As we settle back into our refurbished home, fortune smiles again in June with the visit of a German traveller, Kate Karle. She has been seconded by an American friend who knows us both, a tutor from our writing programme stints in Iowa. Kate is looking for some help and advice about touring the South Island; we happily give her a bed for three nights and quickly become good friends.

This proves to be a real boon over my time in Berlin. Kate has many German contacts. She tells me to get in touch with her again, nearer the time of my departure – she will make sure that I have somebody in Berlin to ease my entry into that world. This is exactly what happens, with her friend Britta in Berlin, and her friends Helena and Manuel in Hamburg (he who would become my meticulous support worker). Kate also promises to act as my interpreter in any later visits I might make in pursuit of the elusive Hasenburgs. With the help and support of Judith Geare at the Goethe-Institut in Wellington and good friends such as these in prospect, the countdown to Germany is on. So begins this journey into a new country, entering first into its language, history and culture. I can hardly wait.

AWAY

FIVE

I Land in Berlin

Note: In the following chapters I use some edited sections from a blog that I wrote while I was on my German adventure in 2014, interspersed with present reflections. As was my habit in the Japanese adventure of April–May 2011, I kept a running diary of encounters great and small, for a sense of freshness in whatever would be later committed to print.

———

NOVEMBER 2014: the German chapter of my life begins. I'm winging my way on board a mighty Airbus 380, via Singapore, a stopover with my son, Timothy, and whānau. I found myself in the company of Germans before I could get out of Singapore: a bunch of teens on a school trip surrounded me, like a flock of boisterous, chirping Teutonic birds. On the midnight flight they soon roosted, while I dozed like a wary owl as the huge jet carved through the air – now still, now turbulent – to land safely and efficiently in Frankfurt. It was simple enough to find the Fernbahnhof and get a train ticket to Frankfurt (Main) Station. I was standing on German soil after a lifetime of reading and thinking about this country; all it had meant in the history of my family, how war itself had given me birth and now, had drawn me here.

The journey from Frankfurt worked well once I found my seat. The ride wasn't cheap at €120, even with the Goethe-Institut discount. I made conversation with Christine, my friendly neighbour, who told me she works selling foodhandling equipment to airlines. Then she asked me how I made my living, so she got the Hasenburg story. At the Berlin station I was helped by another guardian angel, who showed me where to go and how to buy a ticket. People were so kind.

As I had discovered in Japan, there are kind individuals to be found everywhere, those who would erase my deep-seated, baby-boomer conditioning towards former enemies. If these journeys do nothing else, they will unearth a wider sense of belonging to the world the English boy within me needed.

Only two S-Bahn stops to Hackescher Markt and I was at the Institut in ten minutes. I told the interviewer at the school that I was a raw beginner and was too jetlagged to sit the test; he gave in and put me down for Level One. I spoke to Petra in accounts about the cash travel repayment: she agreed it would have been better to have deposited the money in my bank in New Zealand, but some emails had crossed. I hope to get my online German bank account open soon. I sent away all the documents today, and once approved she can deposit the money. As usual, when we travel, there is always anxiety about finance, especially when jetlagged.

I had emailed Konrad Kutt, my host, that I was coming, and he meets me halfway down the street outside Grunewald station. He's a warm, enthusiastic man of seventy-two, with very good English, but he struggles to understand me unless I speak s-l-o-w-l-y. He makes me a coffee and we share some homemade biscuits. He explains how I will be living separately, in a comfortable upstairs room of their house with a view of the large tree-lined garden, in an old established area of Berlin.

With barely time to breathe, we're off again. He takes me walking to Gleis 17, the memorial platform and train tracks next to the present station, where, from October 1941 to March 1945, 50,000 Berlin

Jews were transported to their deaths in the camps. He and his wife Gaby – against years of stubborn resistance, from 1977 to 1998 – had pushed the railway company to create this Denkmal, a memorial and living reminder. Walking around these train tracks with Konrad, reading the embossed records of every Berlin transport to the East and the extermination camps, I am reduced to silence. Back at the house, there is a plaque on the wall outside my room, showing six palms, planted for the Kutts in the Yitzhak Rabin gardens in Israel. Truly, they are Righteous Gentiles. Israel has this designation for all who risked their life for Jewish people in the Holocaust; today, it is granted to those such as my German hosts, who are the guardians of memories.

Konrad and I get on very well. I am absolutely buggered, but have to keep going, to meet Gaby when she comes home and cooks us a meal. She is lovely, warm and friendly, like Konrad, but with her English a little less than fluent. I will have to learn more German, to make it easier for all of us. She prepares a welcome chicken and potato meal, but from now on, she warns, it will be self-catering.

———

As soon as I could I hit the sack, crashing, waking at 2.30am, back to sleep till 5.30am, then I had to stay awake. There was a train at 7.30am, for me to get to the Goethe-Institut by 8.15am. I figured out how to work the shower; with no coffee or any food in my room, I had to wait till I got to the local Kaiser's superette, as the Kutts slept warmly on. To kick my batteries over, I grabbed a coffee at the station and it tasted as mead of the gods. I even tried my German on the girl in the café and she understood me. I asked a fellow commuter which train was coming, even though I knew the answer – trying to speak German as often as I can. I got to Berlin Hackesher Markt station early, had another coffee there, made it to Goethe in time, and saw my name on a class list.

I found Room 102 and met my new teacher, Nicole Brauer, who was very professional (as if there was any other possibility; everything

Fishplate, Gleis 17, 1945: 1035 Berlin Jews, transported to Riga in Latvia.

about the Goethe-Institut would prove to be most efficient). Now it was time to meet the other new students. Those in my class are from everywhere: India to Benin, Brazil to Italy, the great world. Jacopo at my table is from Genoa: I think he's Jewish and so is Rebecca, from London (also at the same table). Jacopo is a rocket scientist who resigned his job in Turin as he was bored (it's true!). He wants to retrain in Berlin in sustainability engineering which is the big thing here, it seems. It will soon become obvious to me that Berlin – Germany, in fact – is a hub for seekers of a new start, a change of career, of direction, as it was for all my classmates. The class is run much like my classes in te reo Māori at home: lots of preparation, handouts, pairs and groups, intense and interactive. The pace damn near killed me! At one point, Nicole was watching me trying to do an exercise and I blurted, 'Please go away, you're making me nervous'! I was so tired – I would never, normally, have spoken to a teacher like this, let alone someone I had just met. Poor Nicole. Welcome to jetlagged learning. I was gasping by 10am, at break time.

I soon discovered that Jacopo and Rebecca were indeed Jewish. Over coffee, a conversation with Rebecca was revealing. She has two

5: I Land in Berlin

'Here lived Gisela Niegho', an infant deported to Auschwitz and murdered there in 1943.

Holocaust survivor grandparents; one is from Hungary. In Budapest, her grandmother was separated from her parents and was somehow overlooked by the fascists. Her grandfather was just a boy, on a train to Auschwitz; for some reason the train stopped, broken down or derailed, and those on board escaped. He jumped off and, in doing so, broke his leg. Those who could run fled for their lives but were quickly rounded up and shot. His immobility saved him; badly injured, he could not move. He hid in the forest – and survived. Jacopo's grandfather had left Hungary before the war and moved to Italy; the rest of his family perished. He escaped the fascist roundup of Italian Jews later in the war, then joined the partisans and lived to tell the tale. I'd come to learn the language; here were two living stories, not to be found in my grammar books.

At the end of the first day's classes, I headed back out to Grunewald to visit the memorial at the station for a second time, on my own, in the light of day. I walked slowly to take it all in, taking photographs of the fallen leaves on the plaques and the wilting roses left by pilgrims. Walking along the station platform, I could see where every transport to the east had been recorded. It is too hard to explain. What post-mortem words, written by an unrelated stranger, can do justice to these cold records of deportations and death?

You say it so easily, it slips off your tongue, fifty thousand, fifty thousand. You have reached the point where words fail and only silence has the power to speak. Turning away, I went home to the Kutts, bearing the first of my many silences.

Even had I not made a point of visiting such memorials, it was still impossible to miss traces of the Holocaust in Berlin. Walking the streets, on the way from the station to the Institut and my classes, I came upon the signs in the pavement. These were the Stolpersteine (stumbling blocks), the cobblestone street memorials. They were laid outside the very door from which the doomed Jewish family was taken, to be transported to their deaths in the waiting camps. They commemorate individuals, outside their homes: I am looking down at Gisela Niegho, an infant who briefly lived, near where I now study German. She was deported to Auschwitz, a babe in arms, in 1943. These visible signs of German repentance bring me up short, and rendered wordless: that she lived here, was stolen away, and murdered there.

SIX

Germany is My Teacher

HERE IN BERLIN, IT IS DAWNING ON ME THAT CULTURE IS BOTH present and past, all at once, in my mind. Culture is not simply external – people, places, events – it is memory itself, the making of memories. I see now plainly how my cultural memory and psychology are filtering the present experience: in trains, in the shower, in the names of places – Wannsee, Potsdam, the Reichstag – even in soap and in shoes. I have arrived here already formed and distorted, into a caricature of balanced vision. It's as if a veil lies over my eyes, as if history is shielding me from – and disguising – the present. Is there any part of my adult life not shaped by this past, bullied and persuaded to filter what is in front of me in my cultures of origin: home, school, community, nation? In all my teenage awakenings – those years from twelve to sixteen before I began drinking heavily – in my mind and my emotions, so open and malleable, I was receiving subliminal images of Germany and the Germans. I am not thinking here of the crude comic-book stuff, where Germans spoke with a limited vocabulary and always had to lose; rather, the images I saw in those adult histories, encountered in my first year at high school.

This came back to me near the station, leafing through one of Konrad's free books from his BücherboXX – a free book project

Konrad Kutt with a BücherboXX.

where repurposed telephone booths in public places are filled with books. It was a book on Jews in the Third Reich: a photo showed a German man publicly shamed and hung with an insulting sign that read, 'I have been a great swine, I have married a Jew'. I suddenly recalled a similar image, in a book in the Blackball Workingmen's Club Library in the early 1960s, at the time the East Germans were building the Wall that would keep the West out and the East locked in. In a faded hardback entitled *I Saw Poland Suffer*, published in Britain in 1941, I saw a picture of a German woman similarly disgraced. Living in occupied Poland, she had allowed her German Kinder to play with Polish kids. She was hung with a sign that read: 'I have been the greatest pig, I let my children play with Poles'.

6: Germany is My Teacher

A German woman pilloried for letting her children play with Poles. Her head has been shaved and she is made to carry a board saying (in rhyme): 'I have been the greatest pig, I let my children play with Poles.'

From *I Saw Poland Suffer* by 'A Polish Doctor', trans. Alcuin, Lindsay Drummond, London, 1941, facing p. 65.

I have never forgotten these words, the record of what happened; but the context and my awakening, the country where I viewed this cruelty was far, far away, in a victor culture, where such victims could be viewed at a distance. The incident was emotive, but remote; the event had no immediate effect on me, a spectator in the humiliation of the woman and her children. This was one of the many shapers of my views on German culture and the German psyche. Apart from the failed attempt to assassinate Hitler on 20 July 1944, it was hard for me to find good Germans. Yet buried in my family history, there was at least one: my mother's half-German cousin 'Pip', Carl Hasenburg's son, named Carl for his father and Ulysses after his uncle. My grandmother told me stories of his Liverpool visits to stay with her, his 'Tante Noonis'; of his arguments with her, in German, and his cheeky comments. She pointed out a statue to him, on a walk, to which he replied, 'Tante Noonis, Du bist ein dummer Esel! Das ist ein Denkmal' – 'You are a dumb donkey! That is a monument!' I never dreamed that this encounter, this memory of fifty years gone by would sleep within me; a family story to guard me against the public shaming and dehumanisation that were so visible in that photograph of the woman and her children.

I was having to call on that family connection to ground me in my time here in Germany, seeking out family stories of my links to a people who, under Hitler, I had felt, were so different to me. Was there really something disordered and evil in the German psyche, that the Nazis had been able to tap into and exploit? There were echoes and twinges: when I rode the rails here; or when I took a shower (as if my own ancestors had never used their gifts for less than humane purposes). Now I was forced to look within at my own crude racial cartoon stereotypes. It was not as if I believed that my country and my ancestors had been any better: on a rational level, I knew enough history to discount such a view. Berlin was awakening my ghosts, those I had not felt so intensely before.

Reminders of the Holocaust disturb images of unreason in the depths of our fears and prejudice. What is now working for me against those forces are the remarkable encounters I'm having with flesh-and-blood people like Konrad and Gaby Kutt. They begin to embody for me this personal, intimate Germany I've come here to experience.

At the Goethe-Institut – which was hosting my every move and every possibility in Berlin – there was nothing but kindness from the staff, especially from Petra Stürmann in the finance office, so patiently answering my every query. As with the Kutts – and their generosity in agreeing to host me in January, after my scholarship ends in December – there was a distinct culture of kindness, that of strangers who were becoming friends and helpers, my Dantean guides. They were leading me gently to the lip of this cemetery of memories on which they must live, that I too might look over the rim, with a more adult view of human nature and of my own complicity in colonial histories. There will be more to say on these wonderful and willing helpers as things evolve, as I try to convey some of my new life's flavour, unter den Deutschen – among the Germans.

Time has moved on, my diary tells me – it's over three weeks now since I arrived and began to fall in love with Berlin, to enjoy the street life and the style of the Berliners. If I struggle with their language in my classes, each day I live a little more like one of them: catching the S-Bahn, arriving at my station Hackescher Markt, buying a coffee at the Steinecke Bäckerei on the corner, making my way down the street to the Goethe-Institut for another day of study. Later, staggering out after five intensive hours of Deutsch lernen, grabbing a döner kebab, I join the crowds of shoppers on Alexanderplatz under the phallic, rocket-age former Communist spire, the Fernsehturm. This television tower, built between 1965 and 1969, is still the tallest building in Germany at 368 metres, with a beacon to warn low-flying aircraft – and, of course, a revolving restaurant. The tower is hard to avoid, all the while appearing to follow you as you wander the busy streets, people-watching and listening to the language.

It hardly seems an act of appreciation to begin my reflections on life in Berlin with an account of a trip to Sachsenhausen concentration camp. This was the first of a deadly series of prisons, interrogation centres, work camps and extermination factories designed to rid

At the entrance gates to Sachsenhausen, Berlin, November 2014.

Germany of anyone the Nazis deemed undesirable, un-German. From the moment Hitler gained power in 1934 and promptly neutered the Reichstag, declaring himself sole leader of the German people, he began to persecute and murder Jews, his political opponents and a range of other victims. Church leaders, prominent intellectuals, artists and writers, gypsies and the gay community, all were targeted. The very worst depths of human nature would be unleashed by Nazism; the rich heritage of German culture – music, literature, philosophy and religion – was about to be decimated. Twenty years earlier, in 1993, I had been to the concentration camp at Terezín (formerly Theresienstadt), in what was still, at that time, a raw post-Soviet Czechoslovakia. The reality of a day spent there had seeded within me, and finally brought me to this place. I was now on my way to one of the earliest established concentration camps – once again, as with Terezín, on a crowded train.

Our histories are always present: a people, a culture, cannot be understood if their past is largely ignored. This was about our shared humanity, about confronting what we all might do, if given the right set of circumstances. I chose to walk from the station, as had the original prisoners of the camp. It was a long march through the town.

6: *Germany is My Teacher*   79

The text reads, 'I am a Hitler boy, the Swastika waves on the staff'.

I did it to remind myself that the citizens of Sachsenhausen – seeing the incoming waves of prisoners, few seeming ever to leave – knew very well what was happening. Two hours passed there: wandering the emptiness, looking at old barbed wire, the signs in German, warning of electrocution for those attempting escape. I felt like a tourist in a past hell: a place incomprehensible, yet one I must approach, come as near as I could, so that the dead were not forgotten and their voices still heard. In the visitor centre, the pictures spoke for themselves: a series of photographs from a display that left me sobered and chastened. Most memorably, there was one of a small boy and his Nazi flag, a local from the town presumably, one of a rising generation groomed for a coming war which would swallow them whole.

Among the books for sale, I was drawn to a remarkable memoir by Otto Dov Kulka, an eighty-year-old survivor of Auschwitz: *Landscapes of the Metropolis of Death*.[1] As a ten-year-old Czech

Sachsenhausen memorial – nineteen Luxembourg police, murdered here in 1945, after refusing to serve in the Nazi occupation force.
AGENCJA FOTOGRAFICZNA CARO/ALAMY STOCK PHOTO

Jew, he was taken to Auschwitz from Theresienstadt and survived seven months in that hell, and the death march when the camp was liquidated. A haunted survivor – later to become a respected historian in Israel – he cried out to his readers that he no longer belonged in this world. All he could express was his alienation: 'The only thing that seems real is my inability to take all this in. Is there something wrong with me!'[2] The horror he feels, for himself and for others, he says, is inexplicable. I have to agree with him. History now seems like an attempt to catch the wind, yet I have this need to try. It's no longer about 'bad Germans'; rather, it is all to do with damaged and damaging human beings, cruelty given full permission and free rein. Could any of us – given the history and the conditions that gave rise to such pathology – become SS guards? That we do not, is it more a matter of grace than of will?

A real-life language lesson. 'Put your chewing gum here please.'
The imperative is followed by the polite form.

Leaving the camp, I'm walking back to the station through the old village with a headful of questions without answers. I wonder if my journey to Sachsenhausen today was to find this man in his book: a voice from that silence, broken by the calls of the black-and-grey Nebelkrähe crows, wraiths that strut over the waste spaces, the ominous guards of an ancient tomb, birds who know something I will never know.

After the journey to Sachsenhausen, it was back to class for more days and weeks of mastering German. There were times when I was just not coping. Language learning in my host country could work very well for me, but sometimes I was not so good in return. It feels a little strange to write about where to put your used chewing gum, but this recounts a small moment of triumph on a bad day for my language learning. We had been studying the imperative form, where an order is given. Then, walking down Barbarossa Straße to meet some friends, I saw a bright-orange rubbish bin with that same verb form: 'Gib Gummi'.

This public message about where Berliners should dispose of their chewing gum gave me a small boost, after an earlier lesson that had begun badly and gone downhill from there. It is not wise to be responding to text messages from home as your teacher begins firing off the first volley of instructions for the day (this applies even if your loved one, on the other side of the world, is locked out in the rain, and asks, 'Where's the spare key?', and you can't remember). I was, in a word, distracted. Jeanette's lost key was not the real cause of my discomfort, though. I am not as good at language learning now – as I feared might be the case – seventeen years after starting to learn Māori at the age of fifty. I have lost quite a bit of top edge since then. Three years plus of earthquake-related PTSD reactivating my childhood stuff has left me a little the worse for wear in the retention of new knowledge, viz, complex German grammar formulations. That was the problem, and I was definitely struggling.

Our teacher believes – probably quite rightly – that German is a more logical language than English (we were learning the komparativ form today). Sadly, my aging brain learned this illogical language as I drank my mother's milk. It seems that these neural pathways deep in my brain consider, rather, that German is illogical, and continually attempt to push Deutsch into Englisch. Te reo Māori within me then slides in helpfully, and provides conjunctions etc, in a process known as code switching. Of course, there are many ways to change from one language to another, but this kind of stress-induced substitution was not a conscious choice – just my brain chiming in. It's all a bit bewildering at times. I know I'm not the only one here having problems; with only two weeks left, it is a bit late to accept the offer of switching to one-on-one coaching. I like my fellow students and I don't want to be a quitter. I managed to buy my Monatskarte for December travel at the Hauptbahnhof yesterday, in an exchange of Deutsch which seemed to satisfy the teller (he didn't switch to English, which is what usually happens as soon as you stumble).

I was learning an existential truth of language acquisition in middle age: the stress of being in a word world where you are no longer the boss. One of the most helpful things that has happened has not been these injuries to my ego – which are salutary – but the experience of feeling lost, confused, angry at times and, at others, wanting to give up and go home. Yes, I'm an adult, leaving middle age; but this doesn't mean I have lost that instant access to childlike states of mind, if the circumstances have rendered me vulnerable and defenceless. This was especially true at the start of the course, when I was jetlagged and for the first fortnight, badly sleep-deprived. I could barely concentrate in the first week and only by the end of the second had I begun to feel remotely human. Mix in some culture shock and those were not ideal conditions; followed in the fourth week by a nasty cold that drained me and is still in no hurry to leave. In other words, stress points, and with such stress comes strong feelings, not always manageable. To all this, add now freezing temperatures, a knife-edge wind, and there is good cause to make a few allowances. My habitual default setting has long been to beat up on myself. Nature took over last week: I had become so overwrought I had to leave the class and flee to the toilet, where I surprised myself by bursting into tears.

I am placing this sequence of events under the microscope to make a point about another group of language learners, whose plight has become so much clearer to me as a result of these experiences. I'm talking about the generations of Māori children in New Zealand, from the mid-nineteenth century well into the twentieth, living mostly in rural areas, after the genocidal New Zealand Wars. They went to school speaking their native language but were forbidden to use it, and were often punished when they did. In Berlin it has become even more obvious to me that language loss in colonised countries must have had multiple impacts: psychological, emotional and communal. What I knew as history suddenly became a felt reality – in no way comparable to the Māori experience, but sobering, to say the least. I had read of this many times and was well aware it had happened. I also knew of the many long-term effects of colonial culture on Māori society. I gave intellectual assent to the sins of my forefathers and also my own, as a beneficiary of colonisation. What I had never *felt*, however, was what it might be like to feel a fool, trapped by your mother tongue, unable to comprehend the language of power.

This was one of my hardest German lessons, and one not meant to be forgotten.

The experience of feeling overwhelmed, unable to understand those strange voices controlling the classroom: confused, angry and wanting to leave, to run, then withdrawing into passivity and, finally, experiencing a lasting sense of failure and worthlessness – all these were carried from the schools to the homes, to the wider society. It is called, somewhat clinically, internalised oppression. The destructive effects of such losses can be seen throughout all colonial cultures of the nineteenth and twentieth centuries. It would set many Māori on a course of generational failure in Western educational systems, at least until recovery began in the 1970s. These wounds still blight New Zealand's image, an indictment that shows up in statistics on per capita imprisonment rates for Māori, compared to Pākehā. At 15 percent of the nation's population, Māori make up 50 percent of those sentenced to prison terms. The role of language loss, of language teaching, of all the cultural losses and deracination so widely experienced by First Peoples wherever Europeans invaded and oppressed, was being driven home to me.

In Sachsenhausen, far from all this, it had become more obvious what race war, what ethnic cleansing, might actually mean. A prison is a prison is a prison, after all, and while there is no direct comparison between the camps in Germany during the Nazi era and our New Zealand prisons today, there is a political, a historical element in this grossly unbalanced incarceration rate of Māori. This speaks of the undeclared war on Māori language and culture that was prosecuted by the settler government on behalf of the European inhabitants who dispossessed and displaced the indigenous people of this land through the second half of the nineteenth century. Here in Berlin, whatever I had come to learn, of my family history, of Great-aunt Lily, some lessons were expected – but others, unsuspected. How amazing then that from the 1960s onwards, Māori have fought back against demoralisation and discrimination, to set in train a true renaissance, a resistance to loss and assimilation. I can never feel what they feel, yet my experience in this language class in the past five weeks has opened the door a few inches, helping me to imagine what it might have been like, having your own words and world stolen right out of your mouth.

Far from my own personal, sobering reflections, with the weekend of 7–9 November coming closer, all the focus in Berlin was on Mauerfall 25. These days celebrate the quarter century that has passed since that historic night of 9 November 1989, when the Berlin Wall miraculously broke open and a new era began for a divided Germany. This was also to be the anniversary of Kristallnacht on 9–10 November 1938, when the Nazi machine unleashed an orgy of violence and terror against Germany's embattled Jewish population, smashing every Jewish window, burning synagogues, and terrorising their victims. Here in Grunewald, in preparation for the coming celebration of Mauerfall, a prior moment of reflection has been arranged to remember this night, involving a march from the memorial at the train station. Hundreds of people were walking silently over the fallen leaves, to the Mahnmal, a memorial at Gleis 17 where the rabbi would call the Kaddish, and we would bow our heads. Young people would stand up and read out the history of that night and of the deportations that followed here in this place. The Last Post would be played, and Hebrew prayers said. This was not the Germany of my imagination – the one fed by childhood memories, shaped by the wounds and fears of my parents – but one of the many contemporary German cultures I was encountering here, in present time.

We marched to the house of the Weimar foreign minister Walther Rathenau, a brilliant Jewish politician who was assassinated by anti-Semitic fanatics on that corner in 1922. Konrad takes me to the gathering, as the police shepherd us along suburban streets in the dusk, past the house of the pre-war Jewish publisher Samuel Fischer. In this stately building, Konrad explains, Hermann Hesse, Thomas Mann and other giants of German literature had come and discussed their manuscripts with their publisher and each other. After the war, the company was able to reform under the direction of Fischer's daughter Brigitte and her husband Gottfried. Günther Grass and Gruppe 47, a group of young writers, began reshaping that heritage in a fresh body of literature, free of Nazi censorship.

Waiting to meet
Elke Rosin.

As part of the Mauerfall celebrations, Konrad takes me to Bernauer Straße for the Lichtgrenze, the light show, where huge light-filled balloons wait to be released along the former sites of the Wall. Konrad says he has an old friend he wants me to meet. He introduces me to Elke Rosin, who as a young woman in 1961 famously escaped from East Berlin after the Wall began to be built along the street where she and her family lived. A photo of Elke and her family in flight went around the world – it was iconic and, for her, would prove haunting. She recounted to me what it was like once they had reached the Western sector with the crowds who welcomed them, and the shock of suddenly becoming famous in the same city, in such a different culture from the one she had grown up in under communist rule. According to the East German authorities, the Wall had been built

Elke Rosin, Bernauer Straße.

as an 'Antifaschistischer Schutzwall' (antifascist bulwark), between East and West Berlin. This was supposedly to keep so-called Western 'fascists' from entering East Germany and undermining the socialist state. In reality, it served the objective of stemming mass defections from East to West. As one such defector, Elke became an object of well-meaning attention; in the end, she was forced to leave Germany because of it. She lived for many years in America, before returning home once her former celebrity had faded over time. In 2014, she was now able to bask a little in that memory, sharing with us her unique experience.

SEVEN

Passing German at the Goethe-Institut

AFTER THE EXCITEMENT OF MAUERFALL, IT WAS BACK TO CLASSES during the day, and my family history searches in the evening. Anyone who has done jigsaw puzzles knows the feeling of frustration as you discover there are missing pieces and nobody knows what happened to them. This is a perfect metaphor right now in my search: last night, another online trawl for the Hasenburgs on German sites came up with the same result. Null. Zero. Nothing. No more than what we already know, which isn't exactly much. We're left looking at a picture, more spaces than pieces. 'Was paßt wo?' (What fits where?) In my language class this week, one of the lessons contained a section with a jigsaw puzzle – we studied a map of modern Germany and learned the names of the sixteen Länder or federal states that make up the Bundesrepublik. Soon, Hamburg and Dresden were fitted into place on the puzzle, and I could see further south, in North Rhine–Westphalia, the area where Carl was born in 1874. The puzzle was almost completed, but there was one rogue piece that just didn't belong in the available space. That was a little annoying, but no big deal; we had to leave it and move on to the next element of grammar: comparatives. Anyone who writes for a living knows about comparisons: language and literature are full of readymade and possible likenesses. Just try getting through a paragraph, like this, without a simile or a metaphor: the words themselves are made of the same material. I need to keep my focus on this experience as a late-life language student: the frustrations of living where you can't understand much at all, but can usually be understood. This might give me a sense of Lily's experiences, in coming to Germany from Liverpool before the Great War and settling into family life with the two Carl Hasenburgs.

She was at least used to change, and travel. I know that she and my grandmother, and their younger brothers, had lived a cosmopolitan life, crossing the Atlantic with their peripatetic father and long-suffering mother several times in their early lives, living on the East Coast of America for long periods. I also know from Bill Honan's research that Hector had learned to speak German, mixing with the immigrants on the New York trams where he sometimes worked. My great-grandfather Peter Daniel had several languages and his sons became linguists, too, in the old-fashioned sense of the word: multilingual. Lily and my grandmother Eunice would certainly have heard German spoken; by the time Lily met Carl and married him in 1898 in Liverpool, she was in contact with the language daily. Once she arrived in Hamburg, she was surrounded and bathed in Deutsch; by 1907, she was well established as a thirty-year-old English woman, now with a German husband and a nine-year-old son, Carl junior. Their second and last child, Anita, my mother's cousin, was born in Hamburg in 1910.

It was plain to me long ago that my Nanny's German nephew Carl was a native speaker of German. Her snippets of story repeated conversations she had had with him when he came to visit her in England about this time, when he corrected her ideas about what was – or was not – a monument. It would be remarkable, then, if Lily had not become a speaker of German at some level of proficiency. She lived through the war years of 1914–18, the Weimar Republic and the Third Reich, until after the outbreak of the Second World War, when she arrived back in England around 1940–41. In 1914, in a country at war with your own, it would have been difficult to have had no German at all. She must have experienced some of my own trials as a language learner. It is with this that I struggle: a labyrinthine grammatical world that my teacher still says is 'more logical' than English. I doubt Lily had access to the language schools for foreigners that exist today. If she had that Bywater flair for other tongues, perhaps she learned her Deutsch in daily life: in the bedroom, in the street and the shops, in the cultural life of Hamburg, now her home.

One thing we do know about her: she was a foreigner with an accent she certainly would not have lost; she would never have quite belonged. We will never know if this was an issue, unless a detailed diary ever emerges. She would have had real periods of adjustment and, surely, loneliness at times, with dreams of home. Now the history-maker comes up against a dead end: a novel is crying out to be written, but not by me. I prefer the blind alleys of non-fiction where it is only the facts that have authority, and the rest is just informed speculation and educated guesswork. Which leaves me where I am now: a sixty-seven-year-old language student, coming to the end of an eight-week intensive course in Berlin, under no illusion as to my fluency. I'm unsure if my quest will bear fruit, unearthing German traces of a long-dead great-aunt, a woman who admired Hitler in his first years in power; seeking those clues while intensely aware of a present Germany revealing itself today. Who, and what, surrounds me now? It seems to make more sense of my great-aunt and her German life if I begin with my own, and those of the others around me, in the present moment. To be working backwards from here to her, eighty years on, fixed on our shared humanity rather than genetics. This will never place me in the family kitchen in the Weimar Germany of 1928, Klosterallee 20 in Hamburg; history, however profound, cannot perform such miracles, it can only pretend to. So much is lost. What is out there to be found, however, needs all the German I now can muster.

On Monday in Berlin, after two months of intensive language learning, there came some very welcome news: 'Herr Jeffrey Holman hat den Deutsch Kurs Erfolg besucht'. I passed my first German course – not with A+ glory, nor even B+, but I passed. All those painful moments in my first week here in November, when I was so badly affected by jetlag and insomnia that I could barely concentrate in

7: Passing German at the Goethe-Institut

My Goethe-Institut Deutsch language class, Berlin, 2014.

English, let alone keep up with the instruction in German. All those feelings of frustration and humiliation when I couldn't grasp the way the language went together, remember yesterday's grammar points, freezing up when our teacher, Nicole, asked me a question. Now, suddenly, it was all worth it. I had achieved a small, personal, German Meilenstein, a milestone, and on reflection, a great deal more. Being in Berlin, I've experienced the stresses felt by the stranger, the immigrant, the traveller, in a language culture not their own, struggling to make myself understood. It's been salutary for me to feel so all at sea.

You will have met such travellers in most Kiwi neighbourhoods: those hundreds of Indian dairy owners who came to New Zealand to find a better life, many with very little English when they arrived. Then there was our Kiwi accent, to make it even tougher. In similar fashion, a strong Turkish community now exists in Germany – descendants of 'Die Gastarbeiter', immigrant workers brought into Germany after the war, to a country that was suffering an acute shortage of workers due to the enormous casualty lists of the conflict. The Turks have accomplished in Germany those things that Indian citizens have, back in New Zealand. They have learned the host language. They have worked hard and prospered, sent their children into higher education and, famously, have elevated the döner kebab into the status of a national icon (I could not get enough of them, walking across town for the best). Immigration can enrich or impoverish, both immigrant and host; it all depends on the degree of openness and, of course, on the very opposite – on prejudice. Both those sides of human nature are in evidence here in Berlin.

EIGHT

Encounters in London Fields

AFTER CHRISTMAS WITH MY BERLIN HOSTS, I FLEW TO ENGLAND, comforted in the knowledge that, on my return, I could continue to stay with them in January. My time at the Goethe-Institut was over, my paid scholarship and board had ended; the Kutts would have been quite justified in saying, 'Time's up, Jeffrey', and waving me Auf Wiedersehen. But we had become friends by now, and my dear hosts had invited me to be their guest for a minimal sum until I flew home at the end of the month. Such wonderful people!

―――

In England, after visits to family and friends, it was back to London for an airport hotel stay. There was research to do at the National Archives in Kew – on Lily's time on the Isle of Man as a wartime internee. I drew something of a blank on this mission but did come up with a file on my great-uncle Hector, all to do with him trying to prove his English nationality! As a spy in the Great War, he had used his faked American identity to move around Germany, while scouting their naval establishments and reporting to his superiors in London. Later, it appeared that it proved hard for him to establish that he was born in London, and that he did indeed hold British citizenship.

I did discover that very few of the German internees were recorded in the Archives' holdings. Help arrived later, in an unexpected venue: 'I think you'd be better off chasing the Isle of Man government sources,' a New Zealand bookseller at the Archives bookshop counter advised me. Grateful, I bought a helpful book from his stock: *How To Research Your German Ancestors*. I left with copies of files from the Archives on Hector Bywater's hassles with the Foreign Office. Will I find anything more in Germany when I go back in a week or so? Will the Hasenburg family rise to meet me from their cold, forgotten graves, or will that edge of the quest be blunted? That kind of speculation is useless and grows best in the dark; better to wake up and write.

The journey so far has often been signs and wonders; now it is time to place my hand in the grip of the unknown. I'm not sure what's really going on, living in 'negative capability', as Keats put it – the need to inhabit and trust this creative tension.[1] It reminds me of how poems will impregnate, gestate within, sometimes for years, until we find the language they have mysteriously prepared for our experiences. Things we were not yet ready to compress and lay on the page, until we hear them in our hearts. I need to stop worrying: can I really forget the immediacy of those weeks in November and December? Better to think of how, when you watch birds for enough years, you have absorbed the movement and the details of a particular species. Then there will come a time, a season, to capture something essential.

———

I won't forget my class members: even though I was concentrating on following Nicole's rapid-fire German instructions in my daily struggles to absorb fresh waves of grammar, these good people imprinted themselves on me. After a few days in England, not having to think or speak in German, Deutsch seems to fly away in strange grey flocks, to roost elsewhere. I won't forget rangy Imad from Benin, locked inside his iPhone beats and his Francophone world; nor Chiara with her da Vinci profile and relentless success with German verbs as I floundered. None of you will be lost, my class of migrating birds, inscribing in me the feeling and the accents of your own mother tongues, combining every day with those of our Deutsch lessons. This intake of a native language by strangers changes us, and we become, if not more like that of our teachers and their culture, then at least shifted from our old foundations to something new and different. A language does not belong solely to its soil of origin; like the culture it creates and that recreates it in turn, language is as liquid, as fluid as water. Words, whole sentences as soundscapes, do seem to adhere to the material world they spring from and have become part of. I miss Germany already, and perhaps more so now because I am missing my Deutsch.

It could as easily be that my search for Lily Hasenburg's German life is all about this: having speech, having writing, being part of one language and literature, and growing into a brand-new world through the challenge of learning another. Who knows? Is this why we adults resist that difficult crossing, because we'll be changed; sensing that our habitual way of seeing, thinking and being must change, begin to die? Listening to some I have met in England and their opposition to Britain remaining in Europe, it sounds quite shocking after being in Germany and hearing Konrad and others express their hopes for continued European unity. They are so aware of the Nazi darkness that overtook them in the 1930s, and of the growing shadow of Putin's aggression in those same territories Hitler tried to conquer.

Long ago, perhaps I may have given unthinking assent to the notion, 'We beat them in two world wars, we won't be ruled by Germany from Brussels, not today!' Au contraire: I am experiencing in Berlin that Germany is a highly successful and advanced modern democracy, having qualities I think Britain is in danger of losing, since the Thatcher–Blair era of neoliberal slash and burn. Germans now possess a healthy fear of ideologues, having come to know the disasters of empire. Who can blame them? To live in clichés of a faded past is seductive. I was lured there once; many of my boyhood dreams instilled in me a prejudice against our recent enemies, the Germans and the Japanese. Going to Japan in 2011, welcomed and hosted by Japanese families, and writing about the kamikaze, began to cure me of those old wounds. Coming to Berlin, I hope the time here in

January is doing something similar within me. Prejudice hurts us, as much as the other person. Does the habitual rejection of Germany and its people help us to live and to grow? Isn't trying to learn their language, history and culture, to understand, to value and appreciate who the Germans are, a more adult response? In the process, as I am finding, learning to love them?

Since living in Berlin, I feel very strongly the need to clean out my stables before I die. I need to throw away old, outworn attitudes and avoid defining myself by rejecting another group of people, based on fear and ignorance. It's time to forget about the last war, however many, bloody wars; if we want to avoid the next one and the next, we must talk to each other and learn to listen. Is it possible to do this if we insist on communicating in our own language alone? Living in New Zealand, learning Māori has taught me that we must be open to each other. So what can learning German, in Germany, teach me?

———

My time in London gave me an opportunity to do some more family research on my father's side of the story. I already knew, from contacts with his children, that my grandfather William Gladstone Holman had served in the First World War in Gallipoli and, later, Palestine and Iraq, and was buried in Mortlake Cemetery, Hammersmith. I had visited the cemetery in 2013 and spoken to the sextons, who informed me that he was buried in a common grave. They directed me to the right place in this huge burial ground: Section B1, Grave Number 64. I had no idea what this meant until I arrived at the site. There was a row of private graves with memorial stones for those who had been able to pay. I discovered that my grandmother did not have the money to erect a grave marker when Grandad had died over New Year, 1948. He was buried on 31 January, only a few months before the postwar reformist Labour government enacted legislation which gave a grant to families on low incomes to bury and remember their dead. Poor forgotten man, who, my mother had years before told me, held me in his arms shortly after my birth in November 1947, and said, 'Isn't

Grandad's burial site at Mortlake: reminders posed in memoriam, on a visit in 2013.

he a lovely lad?'. That is precious. I needed to find him. I wept there at his grave, promising I would do my best to remember him with a headstone, after contacting my UK family members once I was back in New Zealand. This would begin a long saga: I engaged a local stonemason who then went to the gravesite and did some probing: he found a buried plaque for another person, but not my grandfather. Somewhere in the discussion, after sending me images of the site and a selection of headstones to view, he stopped responding to my emails and has since disappeared. The search for my Great-aunt Lily was the key for me; this memorial plan has since languished. I am reminded by this retelling that the work still needs to be finished and have resolved that this time, it will be done.[2]

Back in London, preparing to return to Berlin and the warmth of the Kutt household, I took time out for a midweek service in

St Giles-in-the-Fields, near the site of my old Waterstones bookshop in Charing Cross Road. I needed the silence and the company of strangers. After the service, a trio of worshippers spoke to me outside; they ended up inviting me to a nearby Starbucks, about where Waterstones used to be. As I spoke with the older man on the way, he made some racist remarks about the Japanese. I responded that I'd been there in 2011, doing research, and was warmly welcomed, hosted and helped. 'Burma Railway,' he replied. I figured it was time to give up for the moment, and changed the subject. In the passing conversation, he spoke some German; it turned out he *was* German and came from – of all places – Hamburg. His daughter had not long ago been on a business trip to New Zealand, and we began to make connections. While the others were ordering coffees, we sat and talked. He asked me what I was doing in Berlin. I explained the Hasenburg story – and when I spoke of Lily's wartime internment, the floodgates opened.

In 1938, he had been sent to England from Hamburg with his whole school, when Kurt Hahn – the Jewish founder of Salem School in Germany, and of what became Gordonstoun School in Scotland – decamped and took his pupils with him. His mother was visiting him at the school in September 1939 when war broke out, and she was trapped in Britain. Her husband (this man's father) was in the Kriegsmarine, the German navy: a former judge, his job had become to assess the contents that had been seized as plunder in Kiel. I later discovered that their crews, too, had been interned.

My new friend told me he was sent to the Aliens Registration Office at 16 Bloomsbury Square (which is still there, just a few blocks from where we sat talking); once he had registered, along with the other boys from Hahn's school, they were all sent back to their lessons. He was not seen as a threat, but his mother could have been considered one. However, with her striking blonde good looks and her excellent English with little trace of a German accent, she was allowed to go free, to live in a village more than twenty miles from the coast. Germans who were not sent to the Isle of Man – as Lily was – were not permitted to be what was seen as within range of signalling to offshore U-boats. She wrote to her son from the village to say that she had got him a bicycle, for when he came for holidays. He was allowed to ride around the village, but he was not to go near a certain house where, he told me, 'long-haired men with glasses and sports jackets with leather patches' were living. The implication, he said, was that in Nazi Germany these men – who were obviously homosexuals – would all have been killed.

He had come home to be with her, and avoided that house at first; but by early 1940, he had found that his mother was not only working in 'the house of evil', she was also in the process of teaching the men German. They were working on secret radar technology; he claimed the men never knew they had a German woman for company. My new friend told me he had received a letter from his father in Germany, saying he'd see him soon; he happily showed this to his friends and teachers. None of those who saw it knew the import of the letter: 'After Germany conquers England,' his father assured him, 'there will be a family reunion taking place!'

My friend survived the war, and went on to have a distinguished academic career. Not all of Hahn's German pupils did so: on reaching seventeen, some were sent to the Isle of Man to be incarcerated with the other German internees; others were trained as officers in the British Army and were posted far away, to fight their German relations. Many wonderful musicians spent the war on the Isle of Man, he told me: there was even a future Nobel Prize winner; along with Tiny Rowlands, who later edited the *Observer*.

His stories got one of my other new friends going. He was Jewish, as it happened; hearing of my search, he said he was happy to pass on to his 'expert Jewish genealogist' anything I could send him about Carl, Lily and the Hasenburg children. The last of my new friends joined in, saying his father had spent much of the war in OfLag X in Germany, one of many POW camps for officers. Around that Starbucks table sat three of the congregation from the St Giles church service, each one of them with various, very tangible connections to my unfolding Berlin journey. This gives me faith: life-changing encounters with a higher power at the heart of invisible reality, profound and mysterious meetings unbidden, even unsought. I'd made such a connection with these men; in this revelation, my heart was singing. That trinity of experience, who sat with me, pouring out their hearts, was more than enough to remind me of the eternal moment, the shimmering present. Come tomorrow, I would catch my flight back to Berlin, embracing the here and now.

NINE

Manuel is My Hamburg Genealogist

It was one thing to be in Germany, struggling with late-life language learning. What mattered now was the search for traces of my great-aunt, Lily Hasenburg. I would need help for this: friends, experts – and in one respect, I had come equipped. Kate Karle, whom we had met and hosted back home in New Zealand, would be the next helper, as my German interpreter. We had exchanged messages after her return to Germany. She knew I would be coming to Berlin in 2014, and she put me in touch with her friend and fellow interpreter, Britta Groeger, who worked in Berlin. I met Britta near to my S-Bahn stop in Hackescher Markt, and over a meal, we spoke of my quest. She shared some of her plans too, most memorably, how much she was looking forward to the next Cliff Richard concert! She was a huge fan of this apparently ageless English pop idol, who I could remember topping the charts in 1960s England, and in faraway New Zealand, starring in a series of forgettable musicals. Who knew? On hearing me out, Britta very kindly put me in touch with her close friend and fellow interpreter in Hamburg, Helena and her husband Manuel Petzold. He is a mechanics engineer for the Eppendorf company, involved in research and development; but from my point of view, he's also an expert German genealogist who, in Britta's estimation, would be the ideal person to help me on my quest (as it would prove). Here it was again, happening for me, the right doors opening at the moment of my need. I was feeling both grateful and humbled.

Was als nächstes? What's next in Berlin? I am leaving this marvellous city on the road to Hamburg, in a fast bus on the Autobahn in grey monochromatic weather, passed by speeding Germans and wondering, what's ahead? I plan to catch up with Kate there, along with Helena and Manuel. Sitting here, thinking about this journey, staring out the window, I'm listening abstractedly to two Deutsche Frauen opposite sharing friendly talk, as kilometres unravel, and we pass fields of solar panels. The journey means far more than a €21 round trip to a city I know of only vaguely. It is all about my relatives' lives, up until 1928. Before and after that year, I know so very little: just an old address, Klosterallee 20, Hamburg 37, authenticated in Nanny Eunice's address book entry from that time, tracking her sister Lily and Carl, her former German lover who later married Lily. I do have a business address for him, found recently in an old Hamburg directory entry – 'Rohgummi und Chemik' – rubber and chemicals.

As the kilometres flash by, I begin thinking about what empathy means: what it is like to be German, right now, living with the unavoidable shadow of the Nazi past, as it shades to the present Islamophobia in certain German cities in the former East. Hundreds are marching there right now, in angry protests against immigration policies; all the while, thousands march against them in opposition, confronting this resurgence of fascism and race hatred. At the same moment, in Paris, twelve journalists have been murdered at the satirical newspaper *Charlie Hebdo*, for printing cartoons mocking Muhammad, the prophet of Islam. There is scorn and there is hatred, the very opposites of empathy. I'm trying to imagine what it might have been like for my Liverpool-born English great-aunt Lily to move to Germany with her husband and baby son, just after the turn of the nineteenth century; to live here through both world wars, escaping back to England after France fell in 1940. What were the tensions of being an English woman in the Third Reich, at war again with the country of her birth, as in 1914, caught once more in a crisis of identity?

9: Manuel is My Hamburg Genealogist

Hitler, during Reichserntedankfest, Bückeburg, near Hameln,
3 October 1937. INTERFOTO/ALAMY STOCK PHOTO

What would I have become, had I lived in a typical German household of the 1920s where the father had returned shattered from the Great War and watched, angry, embittered, as the Weimar Republic struggled and finally collapsed under the shock of the Great Crash after 1929? What would I have absorbed, had my family then embraced Hitler and his rearmament programme, still ashamed of the ignominy of defeat, the punitive Versailles Treaty, at the same time struggling in a whirlwind of rampant inflation and the bitter desolation of mass unemployment? Would I have welcomed the Hitler Youth, with its uniforms, its training in military culture, the camps in the country with tents and guns and plenty of good food? Could any boy resist the glamour of the fascist panoply, heralding a return to national pride and prosperity? Would it have mattered to me that the 'troublemakers' – all those communists and socialists – were now to be dealt with in concentration camps? That 'un-German elements' – the assimilated Jews – were to be expunged from the pure Aryan Volk, the German people to whom I could proudly claim to belong?

In my own postwar youth, I was brought up in a victor culture. I would have felt the shame, in one so vanquished, surrounded by parental bitterness. Hitler gave the Germans a new hope and self-belief – at a price. I would have also been affected by the despair and self-loathing in the adult community. In the 1950s and 1960s in New Zealand, we joined Cubs and Scouts, Brownies and Guides; the boys climbed into uniforms and later, at high schools, took part in a Barracks Week all over the country. We learned to put up with the uncomfortable khaki sandpaper suits, the comic drill-squad square-bashing, just to get our hands on the .22 rifles at the range, to fondle real Bren guns we could not fire. Then the seduction of handling killing power, the feeling of belonging to adventure and danger, only ever read about in war comics, in war stories and war films – where Germans were always defeated.

Guns were intoxicating to most of us boys. I could have been a good German, the patriotic soldier. If the chance to fly in gliders had come my way, as the future cadre of the Luftwaffe were groomed and trained to do in secret, I'm sure I would have given my young heart to Hitler. The Nazis knew how to get you. There were families where this was not the case – those I have alluded to earlier – but we cannot choose to which fortunate – or unfortunate – group our history bears us. On this journey, on this very bus, I find myself searching not only for whatever historical remains of the Hasenburgs exist in German repositories of birth, death and marriage, but, for a moment at least, a feeling of being Other: in time, in place, in language and culture. Travelling holds up existential mirrors: my self-image and my past, held up before Germany and the Germans in the present. This becomes an attempt to wipe away inner distortions so that I might come to see, to feel, my shared humanity with a former 'enemy' people; that the real enemy is always ignorance, fed by our fears.

———

The day in Hamburg – walking from the bus stop, arriving soaked at my hotel – got worse when I found my third-floor room was above a busy main artery into the city. My earthquake brain was not going to let me sleep, with the sound of traffic roaring right through the room. I got up at 11pm, went down to the desk and asked to be moved; they kindly obliged and elevated me from 337 to 814. The traffic noise was now barely audible; but the person in the next room was typing on a noisy keyboard, right behind my head. I moved to another bed across the room. By the time I did manage to get some sleep, the night was restless and spoiled.

Kate arrived next morning: my friend from her New Zealand stopover was a professional translator, and now, my beloved interpreter. We caught up over breakfast, then headed off to meet Manuel Petzold. He was waiting at the city's Staatsarchiv, a repository of local and national information. He was quite reserved at first, but he soon warmed to the task of helping this stranger from New Zealand. We sat through an interview with a specialist archivist, who gave Manuel and Kate helpful hints in rapid-fire German. I watched and listened to my newfound allies at work. It seemed that nothing had appeared when the archivist entered 'Carl Hasenburg' in the database, which was no surprise. The last information I had on Carl's home and business here was in 1928; this was the place to start. She gave us a printout of professional researchers, and a Jewish organisation in Hamburg that helps those seeking information about relatives who died in the war. After Manuel tracked down the document numbers we needed to view, we were told we would have to come back to order them on the next working day: tomorrow was Saturday and the Archives would be closed; on Sunday too, when I would be on my way back to Berlin. Manuel told me the documents would be written in the old Fraktur (Gothic) script, which I cannot read, so I would need him with me.

At something of a dead end, we had coffee in the cloakroom, waiting out the stormy gale and lashing rain outside. I did not feel too disappointed – I was aware beforehand that progress might be slow. I asked Manuel about his interest in genealogy. He told me he had 'picked up the habit' from his father, who constructed elaborate family trees while the young Manuel watched. We retreated to a local café, where we shared more about ourselves and our personal histories.

Manuel Petzold, Staatsarchiv, Hamburg, 2015.

We agreed that a sense of connection to local, national and world history makes us aware of a richer tapestry. It was a good beginning in my search for the Hasenburgs in Hamburg.

Manuel departed, promising to seek my relations in old telephone directories of homes and businesses; he's a man with an eye for the chase. He stayed on the case, and was soon sending more material, including the news that my great-aunt's address after Klosterallee 20 – with Frau Bösche at Mundsburger Damm 25 – was authentic, but that this family had left there in 1935, so for now, the trail stops. He'd researched Carl's business addresses in the years from 1923 to 1931, a period of stabilisation in the postwar German economy under the guidance of Chancellor Gustav Stresemann; after Stresemann's death in 1929 would come the disastrous collapse of the recovery, under the weight of the Wall Street Crash and the ensuing global depression. Manuel had searched business directories and found details of the business, Rohgummi und Chemik, which

Carl later operated from home after the partnership, Hasenburg & Lerch (1923–24), had been dissolved. Carl then traded under his name alone, it seems: at least from 1926 until 1931, when the entries end, the firm had been run from the Hasenburg home.

The fate of Carl's business was likely sealed much earlier, after Germany had defaulted on its reparation payments in 1923. France and Belgium occupied the Ruhr; a policy of passive resistance from the German chancellor led to Ruhr businesses shutting their doors, as the government printed the money to pay wages. Hyperinflation was rampant – by June of that year it reached over 114,000 marks to the dollar. According to Stefan Zweig (cited in historian Volker Ullrich's history of the period), 'Abruptly, the mark plunged down, never to stop until it had reached the fantastic figures of madness, the millions, the billions and trillions.'[1] In the teeth of that terrible storm, 'Ullrich shows that the psychological and political effects of hyperinflation were profound', writes Jennifer Szalai in a *New York Times* review. 'Reality seemed to be breaking down. Suffering deepened, along with inequality.'[2] In a left-wing revolt in Hamburg's working-class district of Barmbeck on 23 October 1923, insurgents attacked police stations in the city. Some five years later, after the Weimar Republic had staged a brief and colourful recovery, the Depression tore out the heart of the Stresemann-led 1920s recovery. It would surely be then that Carl's business was decimated, if not destroyed. This could well explain the fact that 'Lillies new address' in my grandmother's book is changed from Klosterallee 20 to 'Bei [c/o] Frau Bosch, Mundsburgerdamm, Hamburg 25.I'. Their home most likely sold, they were now living as tenants. Were they still in Hamburg together, or not? There is no way of knowing now: as we will see, the trail has again gone cold.[3]

Of all things, I then had a dream where I learned that Carl's Önkfeld birth records might be held in the main centre of Wuppertal. Amazed, I told Manuel of this. He contacted the Staatsarchiv in Wuppertal – only to be told he should get in touch with Radevormwald, Carl's actual birthplace. Manuel set things up for me, making a note of what I had to do: write my request to Frau Conrad at the Standesamt, the local registry office. He sent a template letter in German, to forward with a request for the birth certificate (with an English translation, so that I would know what I was asking). The letter read:

> As part of my family research, I need more information about my ancestor Carl Hasenburg, who is said to have been born in Önkfeld in 1874 or 1875. I ask you to send me a photocopy or copy of the relevant entry in the birth register. I am aware of the research fees of 9 euros per quarter of an hour. If you would like payment in advance, please email me the payment information. Alternatively, I will transfer the amount immediately after receipt of the documents.

I love this man! I could now go after Carl the right way around: from birth, not death. I did as Manuel suggested and waited. By this time, there were other delights awaiting me in Berlin: a house concert!

TEN

Grunewald and the Leaping Hare

It was time to prepare for the Hauskonzert that my hosts Konrad and Gaby were organising for the sixteenth of January. I was invited to read some poetry, together with Katsuya Watanabe, a Japanese oboist, and Ulugbek Palvanov, an Uzbek pianist. These amazing hosts of mine were great internationalists. The night arrived, such a marvellous time: at least fifty guests all packed into the Kutts' living room around the piano and a small low stage, where we were to perform. It was my privilege to deliver a mihimihi to the guests – almost certainly the first and last time most of them will hear Māori spoken – and then to read poems from *As Big as a Father*, *Shaken Down 6.3* and a poem, 'The Departed', from *The Lost Pilot*.

The night continued into the small hours. I met our near neighbours, Rainer and Alexandra Gotthardt. I'd already heard Alexandra play piano in December, for the singer Helus Hercygier at a Kurt Tucholsky evening in Halemweg. Rainer is a veterinarian and they had animals of their own, next door. They regaled me with tales of their legendary goose, so I invited myself to visit and meet the great white bird. They told me to come round at 11am the next day. After hearing my poetry, Rainer wanted to buy a copy of *The Lost Pilot*, and I was happy to oblige. The following morning, I made my way

Hauskonzert, Grunewald: Ulugbek, Katsuya, Konrad, me, Gaby, 17 January 2015.

to nearby Winkler Straße 21 – the house almost backs on to the Kutt property – passing the mansions of Grunewald. Rainer's illuminated sign, Tierarzt (veterinarian) made it easy to find; he was on hand to welcome me into the yard. Their massive several-storey house dates to before the war, when his lawyer father owned it, along with other Berlin properties.

Rainer's father had to leave Germany early in the war, as he was opposed to the Nazi regime and was declared unfit for military service. This all emerged as we shared coffee while getting acquainted with Leander, their fifteen-year-old son, who was affecting a deep boredom, though he warmed up as I complimented him on his excellent English. Herr Gotthardt senior, Rainer's unmilitary father, had spent the rest of the war working for a solicitor in Poland – until 1945, when it all changed. It was time for German settlers in Poland to flee back into Germany, ahead of the advancing Russians. In 1939, these Germans had taken Polish lands and properties, as part of Hitler's promised Lebensraum, while the Nazis rounded up and murdered Poland's Jews.

Rainer's father had earlier sent his family to a place near the Swiss border, where they could escape from Germany if the need arose. With millions of fellow refugees, he fled back into Germany from Poland; on the nights of 13–15 February 1945, he was booked into a hotel in the city of Dresden.

Students of that time will know what is coming next: he was woken from his sleep when waves of devastating Allied air raids in those nightmare hours destroyed this 'Vienna of the North' on the Elbe River, killing thousands of Dresdeners and refugees in the resultant firestorm.[1] The city that Lily and her brothers Uly and Hector knew was destroyed, along with many of those they had known there. Herr Gotthardt was far enough away from the city centre to escape the flames that destroyed his hotel. He fled the ashes of Dresden to head south, with the hotel room keys in his pocket. A refugee amidst thousands of others, he was able at last to find his family; they then moved to Freiburg, where Rainer was born. When they could finally move back to Berlin, they found there were strangers in their Grunewald house, including a handyman who had repaired the roof, which had been damaged by a parachute mine. He let them in. Rainer's father also lost properties to the Russians in East Berlin; but as well as their house here in Grunewald, the family were able to reclaim their old city property in Mitte.

Yes, I did get to meet the goose, which had to be restrained from attacking me, as geese are happy to do. Better still, I got to meet Rainer and hear his story. In his work as a vet, he told me, he had been to Peenemünde, where the Nazis perfected the V-1 pulse-jet and V-2 rocket technology, aiming Hitler's 'revenge weapons' at London – that meant at my mother, my grandmother, my father's family, and anyone else within range.[2] As we stood there, the irony – that his people had been trying to kill my people, who were trying to kill his – was hard to escape. Nothing seems personal in modern warfare, but nevertheless, we humans are destroyed. Stories beget stories: if this journey is about anything, it is in liberating and recording tales such as Rainer's which would otherwise be lost or, at least, not heard by an audience beyond Germany.

Hasensprung, Königssee, Grunewald, 19 January 2015.

This coming Tuesday, in forty-eight hours' time, I will be boarding a Berlin Linien bus bound for Dresden, for two nights in this city risen from the ashes of revenge, of memory and, long since, part of my family history.

On Sunday morning I took a walk in the frost to find a church, passing the cold, silent mansions of Grunewald with their massive gates and their signs, 'Einfahrt freihalten' (Keep driveway clear). I came next to Königssee, a small lake bridged by the street named Hasensprung: literally, 'leaping hare'. Sure enough, there were stone animals on either side, gorgeous images of the hare in mid-flight, with the frozen lake as a backdrop. Reaching my destination, I was surprised to see the door of the evangelische Kirche was closed. Martin Luther would not have been pleased. I pressed on. My map showed me there was another church nearby, and after a short walk of ten or fifteen minutes I saw what looked like a church spire, roseate and topped by a rooster. Others were heading there, so it was either a church or, perhaps, a giant poultry farm. It came into view as St Karl Borromäus, the Katholische Kirchengemeinde. The service was underway as I entered, late.

I sat in the back listening to the Bible readings, picking out a word here and there in the German, 'Geist' and 'Gott' being the obvious ones. It wasn't easy to unpick the chanted responses where everything flows together. I was content to sit, absorbed in the atmosphere of worship, then listening to the Pfarrer's sermon. The priest spoke of dreams, citing Joseph in the Old Testament. Almost without trying, I suddenly found myself grasping a phrase: 'Gott kommt oft im Traum – God often comes to us in dreams' – and that was my message for the day. I left as Mass was being celebrated, walking back to Trabener Straße in the dead silence of winter streets, of houses where no life showed at all, and hardly a human voice was heard. 'I've been in noisier cemeteries,' I said out loud to the nobodies who were not listening. I had heard a voice in that church, speaking directly to me. I remembered my dream earlier in the week when the name 'Wuppertal' had come to me. I was thinking that if 'Hasen' meant 'hare', then Hasenburg meant something like 'hare castle' – cod etymology, perhaps? It did seem at times that Carl was leaping ahead of me; once sighted, with a flick of his tail he would disappear over the next rise, perhaps into a fortress. I was hot on his trail, and not about to give up. I would find guidance in dreams yet to be dreamed: that hare on Hasensprung bridge over the freezing waters of Königssee was another omen.

ELEVEN

Taking Old Glory Back to Dresden

MY ATTENTION TURNED TO THE NEXT PART OF THE JOURNEY: Dresden, and the return of the Old Glory flag, passed down from my grandmother. In order to be clear about what I was about to hand over to the museum at Dresden, I wrote a full explanation to accompany the battered, 120-year-old flag, of how my family in New Zealand had come by this historic item, now to be returned.

> **Statement by Dr Jeffrey Paparoa Holman about the 1884 US Flag 'Old Glory' – 45 Stars – formerly flown from the U.S. Consulate in Dresden, until 1912.**

My name is Jeffrey Paparoa Holman and I reside at 173 Geraldine Street Christchurch New Zealand, and I have been living in Grunewald in Berlin since 27 October 2014 on a Goethe-Institut language course and pursuing research for a book on family history.

Both my great-uncles, my maternal grandmother's brothers, lived and worked in Dresden from 1904–1912. My great-uncle Ulysses J. Bywater was the US Deputy Consul General in Dresden from 1906–1912 and my great-uncle Hector Bywater was a journalist there. He was also a spy for British Naval Intelligence from 1911–1914.

These details can all be verified from the biography of Hector, 'Bywater: The man who invented the Pacific War' by W. Honan (1990). I have included copies of documents which give the details of my great-uncles' time in Germany.

I first learned about this from my grandmother's stories: she lived with my parents in New Zealand from 1951, until her death in 1967. She also had brought with her this US flag, which she said her brother Ulysses had taken from the roof of the U.S. Consulate in Dresden in 1917 when war broke out between Germany and the U.S.

She must have got her dates a little wrong, as her brother Ulysses says, in the attached US passport application, dated 15 March 1917 that he left Dresden in 1912, for a similar post in Italy. Nevertheless, I believe my grandmother was correct, that the flag came from Dresden.

This flag, with brass loops dated from 1884, is a 45-star Old Glory and an important reminder that US–German trade relations up until 1917 already had a long history. My brother and I offered the flag to the U.S. Consulate in Wellington New Zealand, and they were not at all interested. My family would like to return the flag to the city of Dresden.

Herzlichen Grüße

Jeffrey Paparoa Holman, Berlin.

My diary entry at the time – 'Old Glory goes home: Dresden has got its 45 Stars and Stripes back' – was recounting the moments of the handover.

These three days – my travel to Dresden and the return to Berlin – were pure gold. Today was one of those peak moments the humanistic psychology movement spoke of in the 1960s and 1970s. I had come to Dresden with a mixture of motives, feeling conflicted, aware that in 1945, the Allies had laid waste a city that need not have been

'Old Glory' – the 1898 flag of the 45 US states, gifted to the Stadtmuseum Dresden.

destroyed. Here my great-uncles and their families had walked and talked, waking each morning of their lives in the decade from 1904 to 1914, when war would descend, destroying the world they knew. I woke up on Wednesday 21 January 2015, a century later, after the bus journey from Berlin with one aim in mind. I was here to return the American Old Glory 45-star flag Ulysses Bywater had removed from the US Consulate as he left for Italy in 1912, taking it with him. Some forty years later, in 1951, his sister, my grandmother Eunice, carried the flag in her luggage to New Zealand to join us, leaving England behind.

Quite how she had come by this treasure, I have no idea. Uly died in 1961, and he had children of his own, two sons. Why would he not pass it on to them? My Nanny is long dead. Why she let us play cowboys with the flag in Blackball, I will never know – unless we borrowed it without asking. The flag flew for a day over our shed, until my father heard a local boasting he would steal it one dark night. Dad told us to bring it inside the house. The flag then went underground, into my mother's care until well into the 1980s, when I let my son borrow it, to pose with his six-gun in our Runanga back yard. That was the end of sacrilege; the banner was folded once more, passing to my brother Eric when our mother died in 2005. We talked about what to do with this flag, with its brass rings dated 1884 – surely the American Embassy would want to have it back in US custody? Eric rang them and they showed no interest.

When I knew I would be going to Germany, I suggested that I should take the flag with me, back to the museum in Dresden. Eric agreed. Old Glory was carefully packed into the bottom of my suitcase and made the 19,000-km return journey to Europe, this time by air. There it lay, until last week, when came time to make the Dresden trip. I had no more research journeys planned and with a week to go before I returned to New Zealand, it was the right moment. Arriving in the city, I found my hotel and caught up on sleep. In the morning, I got up and prayed that the Stadtmuseum on Wilsdruffer Straße would be open to my bequest. It was freezing, a single degree over zero as I made my way through the city, stopping at first to gaze on the Frauenkirche I would visit later. The museum was open, it was a free entry day: nobody around, no security on the door. It almost seemed deserted in the foyer, except for signs of life in the café and bookshop. I tried speaking to the receptionist behind the counter, who had no English at all, which required me to deploy all that the Goethe-Institut had tried to drum into me in those first eight weeks of my stay in Berlin. Needs must: I trawled through my Deutsch, with the odd English insertion when lost for the German word. It worked well enough: she grasped that I had a flag, a donation to the museum. Repeated phone calls brought no response; no one was available to assist me, she shrugged, sorry. I stood there, repeating in my practised German that I had come all the way from New Zealand to bring this flag back. I really could not leave empty-handed. There was only today. She went on through her phone list, as much, I think, to get rid of a nuisance, as she was plainly stressed by this encounter.

Then she brightened: someone had answered, a brief conversation; she motioned me to go through to the café area, to sit and wait. A few

Holger Starke, Stadtmuseum, Dresden, signs the notice of gift for the flag.

minutes later, a tall and very friendly gentleman walked up to me and introduced himself as Holger Starke, the museum historian. We sat together as I told my story and opened the parcel; he could hardly stop smiling. He was amazed and delighted that this flag could arrive from nowhere, at the beginning of his day. I had found my man and the flag had come home. Holger specialises in mounting exhibitions, and he was planning one concerning Dresden's long history in the modern era, of contacts and relationships between the city and the wider world. Since the rupture of those links from the time of the Great War onwards – underscored by President Obama's June 2009 visit to the city, as a way of re-establishing contacts – he was delighted to have an artefact for his future work, pinpointing the moment the breach with America occurred in 1917.

We talked at great length, in a state of mutual satisfaction at the outcome of my journey. We made a commitment to work together in the future, to provide more information about the redoubtable Bywater brothers, and the time that Dresden was theirs, when they were part of a historic expatriate community that flocked to the city, attracted to the nectar of this gorgeous flower. We spoke of what the bombing had done to the city and the people of that world; of what Hitler's madness and Germany's acquiescence in his folly had cost Dresdeners. I felt that in some way, it may have been easier for British survivors of air raids – like my mother and my Nanny – to bury their terrors within a narrative of victory after VE-Day in April 1945. Holger spoke of how the memory of the war was suppressed, hidden in the private and public lives of Germans. It was only in the 1970s, thirty years later, that Germans began to discuss and disclose their experiences as individuals and communities, in a narrative distinct from the shadows of Nazism and war guilt. During this change, the work of such German authors as Max Sebald, published and honoured in the West, has been important in asking us, as descendants of the Allies, to confront the issue of shared civilian trauma, across all combatants and victims. The madness, the terror and the horror of bombing campaigns that were conducted by combatants from every side.

In parting, he gave me a copy of *Stadtmuseum Dresden*, a lavishly illustrated history of Saxony and the city in over 250 objects. I happily signed the release form for the flag; we shook hands, having made each other's day, me promising to return to see his new exhibition in July. *Ars longa, vita brevis* – one day someone will see that flag and wonder just where it came from and what it is doing in Dresden. Whatever notes Holger Starke writes to describe its provenance will only touch the surface of the strange journey this flag has undertaken over the past century to return home.

Back outside in the freezing day, feeling little warmer than on my setting out, I found a restaurant opposite the Frauenkirche where I had something to eat and rested a while. The Frauenkirche, a miraculous cathedral, is famous worldwide for its resurrection and afterlife since being destroyed then rebuilt, post-war, the new stones and the old plainly visible. On entering the massive dome and body of the church, after reading the exhortation to respect the house of prayer, it is impossible to remain unmoved. Small knots of tourists and worshippers stand, kneel or sit in silence. There is no chatter, nothing – at least, until an organist enters the gallery above us, sits down and unleashes a magnificent, swirling volley of baroque organ music, breaking out from some secret place, filling the air, my very being, to the innermost atoms with sounds indescribable, sublime, celestial – and I bow the knee. I pray and give thanks for the city and my journey. It seems almost sacrilegious to think of photographs. I sneak looks at the other pilgrims: none seem to have their smartphones deployed. I spy someone with their phone, snapping, so I take shots of the dome and the organ pipes – discreetly – only to find I have mistakenly switched the phone camera over to selfie mode. There is my visage, framed by a halo of hair, circled by a vision of the dome and celestial light. I move the camera until it looks as if I truly am in heaven, in a moment close to realisation. I am frozen now inside the Frauenkirche of Dresden, here until the end of the age.

Meanwhile, Konrad has sent me a list of Dresden 'must-sees'. The Brühlsche Terrasse is just ahead of me, overlooking the Elbe, as I leave the church. I go that way and promenade, high above the river, in a freezing wind. I walk past the art gallery with its windows painted to express support for migrants and refugees: 'Dresden für Alles, "No One is Ill Legal"'. This is in reaction to the anti-Muslim and anti-immigrant backlash sweeping through many areas of Germany, here too in the East where unemployment is high. Islamophobia is taking root in the hearts of blue-collar conservatives, stoked by right-wing factions like Pegida, the anti-Islamist group in its Dresden home. There's a banner hung over the entrance to the art gallery with a quote from Goethe: 'Das Land, das die Fremden nicht beschützt, geht bald unter' (The country that does not welcome and shelter strangers will soon go under and fail). This debate is deeply ironic: in a monograph, *The English in Saxony*, that I bought at the museum and am reading over lunch, it is clear that both railway engines and spinning jennies – machines that were at the heart and soul of the Industrial Revolution – were brought to Germany from England. Saxony's industrial economy arrived from elsewhere, carried by outsiders. History's ironies once more: 'Dresden für Alles', indeed.

I look at a map of the city's points of interest and see there is an Erich Kästner Museum – named after the author of *Emil and the Detectives* – across the river at Innestadt, the old city. I make my way shivering across the bridge spanning the Elbe, opposite the Catholic cathedral, entering what was formerly East Germany. A good walk, time to notice there are far fewer shoppers here than over in the glitzier new town. The old Ossi-era flats have a tired air about them. I see numbers of small-framed elders, wandering the empty boulevard in grey, muted garments. I'm wondering if the echoes of a broken Nazi state, then a hard-nosed Communist regime, live on in the bones of their lives. I find The Kästner Museum is undergoing renovations, but I'm still able to visit their bookshop and café. I sip an espresso while admiring my purchase: *Emil and the Detectives* – in German, of course. By now it is 4pm and the sky is already darkening; sightseeing is over for today. Recrossing the Elbe, making my way back to the hostel, nourished on that remarkable meeting with Holger, I reflect on how we are all just a little bit more German than we probably suspect.

By Thursday, back in Berlin, I was getting ready for a trip to Wolfenbüttel with Konrad and Gaby, to show me around the famous Herzog August Bibliothek and the Lessing Museum nearby. I was probably a bit worn out for another big day on the road; it was stressful at times, but well worth the journey. We passed through what were, until 1989, the two checkpoints Berliners had to get through if they wanted to visit West Germany. My hosts remember the Cold War only too well. In 1969, Konrad was hired to work in the Ministry of Education in Berlin, the first federal ministry, inside the encircled city (since 1949, Bonn had been the provisional capital of the Federal Republic of Germany). Moscow was enraged; the Russians responded to this 'provocation', flying MiG jet fighters over the city, right above the ministry building, breaking the sound barrier on high, in a pointed message that they were not to be trifled with. We may forget about this time, when so many fingers were on hair trigger; but Konrad has never forgotten the tension Berliners lived through, before Mauerfall in 1989.

Back from the Bibliothek in Wolfenbüttel – a bibliophile's heaven of ancient printed and handwritten manuscripts – and delighting in a snowfall that whited the town, I was ready for Sunday and a trip to the Grunewaldkirche with my next-door-neighbour friends, Rainer the veterinarian and Alexandra, his pianist wife. The service was to be recorded for radio and the priest had emailed everyone to please come and fill the church. Reading and singing in church was good for my German. During his sermon the priest mentioned more than once the name of Dietrich Bonhoeffer. Rainer and Alexandra explained that the young Bonhoeffer had been confirmed in that same church with his sister in 1921; the family had lived nearby in Wagenheimer Straße 14, where I determined I would go. As a pacifist theologian, Bonhoeffer had confronted the Nazi evil head on and paid the price – death by hanging – in 1945, when the war was all but over. His memory is a shining star in that long night of darkness. There is no human society where we can escape history, or its lessons, but in Germany today, there really is nowhere at all to hide from the shadows of Nazism.

My final Berlin visit is to a site of great interest: Teufelsberg, a famous Berlin hill that was the site of a listening station run by the American National Security Agency during the Cold War to track Soviet-bloc communications. Post-war, it kept watch over what Moscow and its satellites in the East were up to. Today, it is a graffitied ruin. Abandoned, sold to developers after the Wall fell in 1989, it has proved a major commercial failure, as none of the projected apartments were completed and sold, its promoters went bust and the spraycan tribe moved in. This Cold War citadel was begging to be sprayed and tagged. There was no easy public access by the time of my visit in January 2015. There is a locked gate and a live-in couple who are paid to act as caretakers. Rainer, as a vet, has privileged access; he looks after the three dogs that guard the fort these days – a Rottweiler, a Dobermann and a little Schnauzer. A phone call to the guardians and we drive straight in, taking a guided tour through a labyrinth of dark concrete corridors and cold, bleak stairways. Every

Rainer and Alexandra on the roof of a graffitied Teufelsberg, 2015.

available surface is choked with graffiti: it's hallucinatory, as if the set of a dystopian epic, like Cormac McCarthy's *The Road*. We make it to the top: freezing, looking out not on Berlin but a blanket canvas of swirling mist. Spooky does not cut it.

Then it was time to go within and find the dogs to give them their injections. The caretaker and his partner live deep inside the Minotaur's cave – a pair of postmodern techno-hippies. I can still see the couple in their virtual reality bubble. You would have to love the lifestyle to survive up there in winter. But the coffee was great and the atmosphere in the bunker was truly out of this world.

As we left, Rainer pointed out to me a small series of what looked like porcelain figures, white flowers on the wire that upheld them. He told me this was a memorial to the Trümmerfrauen, the German women of Berlin who cleared the rubble away, by hand, after the Allied bombing campaign levelled their city. This was important for me to understand, he explained: that Teufelsberg (devil's mountain)

Trümmerfrauen at work, clearing bomb damage.
AUSTRIAN NATIONAL LIBRARY/INTERFOTO/ALAMY STOCK PHOTO

was a man-made elevation, built from the ruins of what was once Berlin. Eighty metres high, it consisted of 20 million tons of broken stone, brick and concrete, trucked there from the war's end until 1972. The Americans built their spy base right over it, above a site where Hitler himself had laid the foundation stone of a never-completed military school. This was Berlin's wartime graveyard, the end of Hitler's dreams. It was a place of silence and reflection, shrouded in mist.

The day of farewell was coming nearer. Teufelsberg was a good place to end my journey, overlooking a city and a people I have come to embrace in the past three months, upending old stereotypes, showering me with goodness and human stories. 'Berlin! Berlin!', as the writer and satirist Kurt Tucholsky saw it, was a place to be neither resisted nor ignored.[1] I made one more visit, standing silent before Dietrich Bonhoeffer's house in Grunewald. My prayer was for them, my German family.

The final mission as I wandered the city, a day or two before I left for home, was to the Swiss Embassy to get a contact for the

Konrad and Gaby Kutt, Grunewald, my peerless Berlin family.

Swiss Red Cross. I was given an address for the chargé d'affaires in Bern. I wrote before my departure seeking any help that might shed some light on Robin Bywater's letter to me in 1990, in particular, his claim that 'Uncle Uly managed to get Lily out of Germany through the Red Cross; that she was interned on the Isle of Man'. Back in New Zealand, the search would go on; with Manuel on the case, together we would again pick up the trail.

Dear Konrad and Gaby, how can I thank you? This was uppermost in my mind, packing on the morning of departure. Their house, an island of light and culture, delivering me in love and kindness from the poison of my childhood brainwashing in postwar New Zealand, a victor nation with the power to shape a winner's narrative in my child's mind. War comics, war books, war films: none of these had much room for anything good about the Germans – or the Japanese. Even as an adult, that poison was deep within me. My beautiful Grunewald hosts were setting me free.

TWELVE

Certificates of Birth and Death

Leaving Germany was never going to be easy. I'd made some strong attachments and felt strangely at home. I knew Konrad and Gaby would be feeling it too, after the three months we had spent together, living side by side. When I woke on the final morning, Konrad was gone, a note on the table saying he was going to look after their grandson Robert and would be back by 2pm to take me to the airport. Gaby was there and we shared breakfast; she would leave at noon to take over the childcare duties and Konrad would return, as my taxi to Berlin Tegel. It was a loving conversation, winding down to a goodbye both of us hoped would not be final. I got to hear a little more of her story, from her early career in nursing, after dreams of being a doctor, to a life-changing decision to train as a lawyer, where she spent most of the rest of her working life as a legal advisor in the trade union movement.

The subject of the war came up again – it is never far away, acknowledged or not, when talking to this generation of German baby-boomers. She told me of her dear friend, a 90-year-old rape victim whose wounds reach back to 1945 and the arrival of the Russian victors in Berlin. She was raped by Red Army soldiers, as were thousands of other German women who cowered in their basements, waiting for the worst. Her salvation from more abuse came from an unexpected source: a Russian officer arrived, demanding to know who the rapists were. This relief then turned ugly: after pointing them out, she and the other women had to watch as the officer ordered their summary execution. She has carried ever since, along with scars of her own violation, feelings of guilt that these men were shot when she identified them. Gaby told me that this elderly woman still has no peace, that the war for her will only truly end when she dies. Seventy years on from Germany's surrender in 1945, it is still alive for those who were brutalised, regardless of right or wrong, or to which side you belonged. As I thought of these women, I felt my mother there with me.

When the time came for Gaby to go, she came to my room and we embraced. Farewelling me in German, she said, 'Ihre Zeit hier war eine Bereicherung' – your time here has been an enrichment. This was the same expression my friend Britta had used a few nights earlier, as we were sharing a meal with her friend Samer and saying our goodbyes. I assured Gaby it was the same for me, then watched as she cycled off down the path. I waited for Konrad to come back, with more than a touch of Reisefieber kicking in. I travel so-so: I leave badly, always wanting to be at the airport early. Konrad, on the other hand, is the soul of delay and distraction. He takes his time, never seems to be in such a hurry that he cannot stop and smell the roses. As the clock ticked, he was happy to sit and talk. I just wanted to go. We made it in plenty of time, of course, managing to keep my demons at bay. Konrad came right into Departures with me, standing at the Air Berlin counter while the woman on check-in, her tattooed arms visible through a white blouse, compared notes with me over my John Pule tatau designs. Konrad seemed quite amused by all this body talk; I could see he just didn't want me to go, avoiding the inevitable goodbye. I gave him a final hug and joined the queue for security.

What a remarkable man he is: born in 1941, into a Germany whose rulers were carrying out what would become history's most infamous genocide; living to see the seventieth anniversary of the liberation of Auschwitz. He was only three years old when the guns began to fall silent; now, a Berliner who does everything in his power to heal those wounds. Konrad, my dear German friend, you are the very best of men, truly righteous. I will sorely miss you.

The flight from Berlin was bumpy, but the Frankfurt landing had a smooth patch. At the Singapore Airlines check-in, another woman with tatau – not quite visible – noticed mine. That started a conversation, so she was given the full story, with pictures. I had to explain the Welsh dragon (my ancestry) and the Latin tag with the three crossed trumpets, symbol of my father's wartime aircraft carrier, HMS *Illustrious*. God alone knows what the queue behind me was thinking. She sorted out some issues: my New Zealand passport was less than six months to expiry, and my British–EU document had no visa stamp. Between Frankfurt and the next two long hops to Singapore and Christchurch, it was a slow, sleepless dream that would end with me stepping back onto Te Wai Pounamu, in Christchurch, one changed man.

———

Early in 2015, back home just on a week now, adjusting to the insanely surreal colour of this brilliant 4D light and high heat after the grey palette, the invisible skies and cold, cold air of Berlin. I revel and stagger: this is more than jetlag, more than culture shock. It is as if I have been bodily to a place where once I was present only in my imagination. I have travelled to that Germany of the mind – a crudely drawn landscape, cities known only by their names as bombsites – a people and a culture frozen into 1945. I have stepped into those photographs, that tired old narrative: it moved, shivered, springing to life, wrapping me up in a seventy-year timespan of change and renewal. Once there, in the present moment, Germany was German people: the lives I became entangled with, breathing colour and reality into black-and-white images carried over the border of time, landing at Frankfurt in October 2014. Three months had altered everything: the changes within me felt deep.

Then something else changed: a letter arrived from the Standesamt, the civil registry in Radevormwald, with Carl Hasenburg's birth

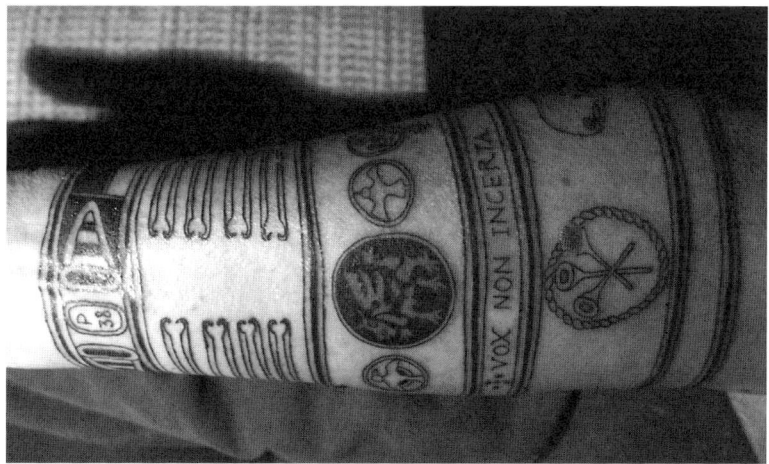

Tā moko, nā Chris Harvey he mahi tohunga tēnei, my family history, by a Tūhoe expert.

certificate enclosed. That was quick: I'd posted my application only a week or ten days before leaving. Manuel's help was proving invaluable, and I would need him once more: I could not read the longhand German entries from the 1870s. I scanned the certificate into a PDF file and emailed it to him in Hamburg; in two days, a translation – and my answer – was back.

> I'm happy for you that you received the birth certificate of Carl Hasenburg. Thank you for forwarding it to me – I have to admit that I was curious too. First of all: yes, it seems they didn't charge you any fee for their service. Secondly: What a surprise! You ordered the birth certificate and got also his date of death! For the details, please read my transcription and translation that I attached to this e-mail. It seems that he died a natural death and was not killed by the Nazis. What amazes me even more is that the name of Wuppertal that appeared in your dream obviously had a meaning. Enough for now – this will give you some material for contemplation.

If Manuel was surprised, I was shocked. Sitting in a café, looking at what he had written, opening the documents, reading his transcription of the German text and the translation, one story was dissolving before my eyes as another unfolded. There was Carl, at the bottom of the birth certificate, quite clearly stamped, '*Gestorben*': 'Died 9.5.1954, No. 46/1954 Wuppertal-Beyenburg'. I could see where his father, also Carl, a thirty-one-year-old farmer, had registered the birth on 16 September 1874; that his mother was eighteen-year-old Emma Höller; that our Carl had been born on the ninth of the month – all of this overshadowed by the fact that he had not been killed by the Nazis during the war, as Robin Bywater had written to me. Was he even Jewish? What the hell was going on? I had relied on that scrap of history for so long, no reason to doubt it; now, another explanation was needed in the story. I went home and reread Robin's 1990 letter: 'Needless to say, I will be very pleased to meet and talk with you and hear what happened to my dad's sister, Aunt Lily Hasenberg [sic] and her son after World War II, *as I know her Jewish husband was murdered by the Nazis* [my emphasis]. I know Uncle Uly managed to get her out of Germany through the Red Cross and she was interned on the Isle of Man, but I never knew what happened to her afterwards.'

All sorts of explanations now spun around in my head. Were Lily and Carl separated before the war? Did she remarry, or live with another man, who was Jewish and was later killed? Did she make up a story to get out of Germany, and when did she leave? Did Uly make this up and tell Robin later (he was good at that) – but if so, why? And if the second half of Robin's account was correct (her internment on the Isle of Man), then why not the rest?

In the gratitude that flowed from knowing where and when Carl had died (there was no doubt this was him), there was also the wonder of my January dream back in Grunewald, where the name 'Wuppertal' had come to me, after my first visit to Manuel in Hamburg. It truly was as the priest had said that day in the Catholic service at Königssee, 'Gott kommt oft im Traum' – God often comes to us in dreams. This was what had sent Manuel searching for Carl in that same area, leading us to this information. Whatever the truth is – whatever we can establish as a fact – there is now a grave, and a fresh story to follow in the city records of Wuppertal. This may reveal more of Carl's life, after he left Hamburg to return to his place of birth; and more, too, of what had happened to my great-aunt Lily, to my blood relation, my still silent ghost.

THIRTEEN

Victor Culture and Colonial Amnesia

ONE WEEK ON SINCE DISCOVERING THE ACTUAL CARL Hasenburg did not die in the Holocaust, I'm still troubled by who gave Robin Bywater his information, and who it was talking about: 'I know her Jewish husband was murdered by the Nazis.' His claim, too, that Uly managed to get Lily out of Germany through the Red Cross, I'd assumed he had heard from Uly himself. Conversations with my counsellor at the time threw up a number of possibilities. Believing the story as it came to Robin from Ulysses: was this his uncle's distractive technique? A better story than the truth? A story needed at a particular moment, told then for a reason, and handed down? I'd been grappling with assumed facts, which could well prove to be fictions. My great-uncle – the only person who could have told Robin this story – did not die until 1961. That account was still uppermost in Robin's mind when, in 1990, he wrote to me about my grandmother's family. It was true for him, true in the sense that he believed what he was told. There can be no doubt he knew that story; either my great-uncle told him a lie, or he'd heard this from another family member – though that is most unlikely. Uncle Uly would certainly have known Carl Hasenburg wasn't Jewish. He would certainly have met his German brother-in-law-to-be, when his sister married Carl in Liverpool in the late 1890s. History is more slippery than ever in the hands of the dead. Time now to focus the historical record, until something other emerges.

One thing is clear: there are Hasenburgs living now in the immediate vicinity of Carl's birthplace, Önkfeld, and his burial place in Wuppertal, an area known as Oberbergischer Kreis and nearby Märkischer Kreis. Manuel has followed up the last message with a series of links, one of which shows the geographical extension of surnames in Germany, based on entries in current telephone books (at least thirty names here). Another shows a possible relative back in that time: Ernst Hasenburg, born in Önkfeld on 1 October 1880, who died in battle in August 1917 – 'at least a cousin, if not a brother of Carl', Manuel writes. This gives me hope that somewhere in Wuppertal or its environs is a relative who may know something of the family history. The note of Carl's death in 1954 (sent with the birth certificate) locates his grave at Wuppertal–Beyenburg; buried in the Evangelische Kirche, the Lutheran church, an unlikely resting place for a Jew – unless he had earlier converted to Christianity, or even, perhaps, was in denial about his identity? It seems unlikely.

Whatever else this search for historic family relationships throws up, there is an underlying thread that keeps emerging: influenced by and linked to Germany and its people are the English and, by extension, those of us who live in England's former colonies and dominions. It is not simply that I have relatives with German connections; rather, that we are all in some way affected by Germany's place in history. From Gutenberg's development of moveable type (whence mass literacy became possible) to Germany's lead in developing jet flight (mass travel), there are multiple, diverse strands entangling the West in this unfolding German narrative. The radical breach from 1914 onwards – the Great War and its continuation, one generation later, in Hitler's war of aggression – has blinded many of us to Germany's pre-existing place in European, Western and colonial cultures, its history and influence from the last war's end to the present day. Before 1914, Germany was a strong European trading partner worldwide; the presence of my family members in Dresden in the first ten years of the twentieth century, as well as Carl Hasenburg's much earlier arrival in Liverpool in the 1890s are all signs of these relationships. It has come to light only recently that Hitler's half-brother Alois lived in Liverpool, at least from 1911, with his Irish wife, Bridget Dowling. She later claimed that Adolf Hitler himself moved there in November 1912 and stayed with his family, before returning to Germany in April 1913 – though her account is now regarded as extremely dubious.[1]

Germany was at the forefront of the Protestant Reformation in Europe; coalescing into a national entity in the nineteenth century, it became an important consumer of the technology and the products of the Industrial Revolution in Britain (as I discovered on my visit to Dresden). Germany's philosophers and theologians, based in old, established universities, were transforming our views of God and man. Prussian unification gave rise to a militarism that would become for many, after Bismarck, the primary identifying marker of the German character. The country's imperial ambitions were no better, no worse than any of those European powers with whom it would eventually contest regional, colonial and world dominance. German immigration spread its ideas and influence, especially in America; the best of its scientists, musicians, artists, writers and thinkers enriched the world. Today we see Germany holding a central place, maintaining the peace and prosperity of Europe; yet the Nazi era remains in the wings, a darkness hovering over present light.

Living in a so-called 'victor culture' post-World War Two has shaped our vision. Germany has existed in our memories as a vanquished state, shadowed by the unspeakable crimes of the Holocaust. We may concede that there were those few 'good Germans' who resisted Hitler, while remaining unaware of what has long been good, and great, about this nation and its people. We know the negatives: what is on the other side of the ledger? What do we owe them? What can we find in Germany, past and present, that allows us to identify with a shared

Opposite: *Trains to Life, Trains to Death*: bronze sculpture of Jewish child deportees by Frank Meisler, Friedrichstraße Bahnhof, Berlin (detail).

and flawed humanity? These are the deeply troubling questions many Germans have been struggling to answer from the war's end until today: who they were as a people, what did they become, and why? For those of us descendants of the wartime Allies, how can we come to terms with the war and its annihilation of a recognisable, prior German civilisation, one that by the mid 1930s had clearly lost its way, in thrall again to militarism – and to fascism?

Looking into history's mirror, this may seem like a 'What's it got to do with us anyway?' kind of question. But we do not have to look far into the colonisation of New Zealand and the wider Pacific to see complicity. We see unjust and illegal aggression toward tangata whenua and tangata Pasifika – plainly, there exist historical crimes. We see land confiscations and the ongoing effects of cultural imperialism, all needing to be addressed and atoned for. We have much to learn from the German experience, in a journey of repentance, redress and reconciliation. It was not only Germany playing the deadly game of colonial master in Sāmoa in the nineteenth and early twentieth century; our inflated ambitions in that domain had fatal results for the Sāmoan people. What makes one invader any more morally palatable than another? Is it who controls the writing of the story?

It was only our puny size that made us a less damaging presence at the time. Is it just to be a numbers game, when any human life is taken by an invading power? Will the scale of state-sanctioned murder be judged by how many, or how few were killed? Eleven Sāmoans were fatally shot and fifty wounded by New Zealand police on Black Saturday, 28 December 1928, while demonstrating in Apia against the harassment of the Mau independence movement.[2] This may not seem the same level of crime against humanity when pitted against the staggering numbers murdered by the Nazis; but in the scales of justice, where is the difference? As colonisers of Sāmoa, we have shown the same racist and genocidal tendencies, when giving them free rein. In spite of then Prime Minister Helen Clark's formal apology in 2002 for 'mistakes' by the administration at that time, it seems we would very much like to forget and to bury such crimes. Germany, though, has had to face facts.

There are other forms of erasure that do not go to such inhumane extremes as concentration camps and gas chambers. Pākehā/Pālagi New Zealanders have a record of cultural and linguistic suppression in their colonial histories. It was not simply the crude supposition held by many settlers in the late nineteenth century that Māori were a dying race. When they did not oblige by dying out as predicted, their language and cultural norms were systematically repressed, and exoticised as window dressing. An existential threat to Māori ways of being promised a lingering death of their history, their culture, their mana as First People. Since the 1970s, however, as part of a worldwide movement of decolonial revolution and evolution, many Pākehā New Zealanders are beginning to move beyond this old war on Māori difference, and necessary advances are finally happening. Yet the history remains, the tensions live on in a slow and painful resolution. Given any kind of reason, racism's so-called 'silent majority' will make their views heard.

Germany, too, has tried to confront its disastrous embrace of fascism, to rebuild the viable democracy that failed in the Weimar Republic. It would be salutary for New Zealand to learn how they have done this, and what it took to face that past. The Hitler regime was monstrous, but its ideological underpinnings were not unique. Racist and eugenicist thinking, justifying murderous practices, was everywhere common in the 'civilising' West in the colonial era – including the colony of New Zealand. Names as illustrious as Charles Darwin, Sidney and Beatrice Webb, Winston Churchill, George Bernard Shaw, H.G. Wells, Harold Laski, John Maynard Keynes and even William Beveridge, key architect of Britain's post-1945 welfare state, all figure in a roll call for the eugenicist movement. There was no place for the weak and defective in the progressive utopias of left or right. Hitler, now the leader of Germany's fascists, had long been an enthusiastic champion of eugenics. Under his dictatorship the Nazis would simply, brutally, put euthanasia into widespread practice.[3]

The eugenics movement in America expressed itself early in immigration laws, from the 1880s onwards: an 1882 Act prohibited entry to any 'lunatic, idiot, or any person unable to take care of himself or herself without becoming a public charge'. The laws were extended in 1907, denying entry to any who were 'mentally or physically defective, such mental or physical defects being of a nature which may affect the ability of such alien to earn a living'. Compulsory sterilisation of the 'unfit' began in Indiana in 1907, and other states followed. A Supreme Court decision in 1927 upheld America's right to enact this kind of legislation to 'prevent our being swamped with incompetence'. The Nazis looked on in admiration, and when they enacted their own eugenicist laws in 1933, they were still behind the 'advances' made in the West, by those who would later judge them at Nuremberg. German doctors, accused of murdering people, argued in their defence that they were only putting into practice ideas that were widely accepted in those same democracies that had defeated them. New Zealand was not exempt from this, with the notable exception of Ivan Sutherland – a vigorous opponent of the racist eugenics movement and a champion of women's rights, who fought for the acceptance of Jewish immigrants from Germany in the 1930s. His entreaties were spurned.[4]

The question of who will bear the heaviest loads of guilt in history is next to insoluble, but the issue of human likeness, as opposed to cultural and historical differences, is not so hard to address. What confronts me, in this exploration of family history, is what I have in common with the Germans of yesterday – and today. What bound us together in that era, when my ancestors married into German society, living and working among the Germans? What Germany had to offer then – what it has to offer us today – is at the heart of this journey into the country of the dead, our common destination. This is revealed in Robert Graves' classic memoir of the Great War, *Goodbye to All That*.[5] The opening account of his family tree looks like dry stuff; but my ears pricked up when I saw his family on his mother Amalie's side were German – von Ranke. Her father (Robert's grandfather) had fled the country after getting into trouble during the 1848 revolutions, and landed in England. He went on to serve as a surgeon in the Crimea, and married into a London line of expatriate Danish. By the myriad ironies of history, Amalie would give birth to a poet who would later become an enemy of his father's German relatives, in 1914.

There is no way of knowing how many relatives from opposing sides faced each other, or had a hand in killing their close kin. But there is no doubt it happened, as Graves makes clear: 'Among these enemy relatives was my cousin Conrad, son of the German Consul at Zürich. In January 1914, I had gone skiing with him between the trees in the woods above the city,' he writes, remembering the last days of his childhood as he finishes Charterhouse school. Before the year's end, he will be lining up to kill his cousin. He tells of how gentle Conrad, who had 'strong feelings about shooting [animals]', went on to serve 'with a crack Bavarian regiment', win the Pour le Mérite and, after somehow surviving the war, as did Graves, was murdered by 'a party of Bolsheviks in a Baltic village'.[6] One minute you're a child playing with your cousin; the next, you're grown up. The guns are real, you and your comrades are shooting at him; he and his are firing back at you.

What of my grandmother Eunice? In the early 1900s, she is showing her beloved nephew Carl around the charms of old Liverpool; yet at some point in the years 1914–18, we find her supervising the manufacture of high explosive shells to be fired at his father's people. Carl Hasenburg junior was nineteen years old when the war ended; his father was forty when it began. It is possible that one or both of them saw some form of service: that the Bywater sisters had fought a proxy war, through their menfolk. What was it like for Lily Hasenburg, Eunice's sister, to go through this war as an alien citizen? Can we see her there in 1914, surrounded by cheering Germans in the great seaport of Hamburg, alight with the prospect of going to war against their English rivals? Can we imagine how she felt?

FOURTEEN

English Lily in a German War

Although there is little information, so far, as to what happened in Lily Hasenburg's life once she arrived in Germany after the turn of the century, we know that Carl went back to his job as a rubber company manager in the Hamburg area. The city had been a developing site for the rubber industry since the founding of the Phoenix Rubber Company in the 1850s. With the arrival of early automobiles in the 1890s and, soon after, the development of pneumatic tyres, as well as diverse items from rubber overshoes to military observation balloons, and for all manner of weapons and their transportation, rubber was fast becoming a vital strategic material – so much so that the belligerents continued trading with each other even during hostilities, in order to obtain supplies. Germany provided Britain with its precision Zeiss binoculars, in return for deliveries of rubber. Can anything show more clearly than this the insanity of war?

I have tried to imagine Lily living in Germany and settling into her new life in Hamburg. However much German language she knew before she arrived, she would need to acquire more. Ulysses and Hector, we know, were confident linguists and were living and working in Germany, in Dresden, between 1904 and 1909. Both married and had children while residing there – so Lily had relatives close at hand. Only my grandmother Eunice, of the four Bywater children, was still living in England. In these early pre-war years, we know that Lily sent her son to stay with his aunt Eunice in Liverpool, giving rise to those family stories recounted earlier. From the royal family down, a wide network of personal relationships now linked the two countries. In 1910 Anita, the second of the Hasenburg children, was born in Hamburg; like her older brother Carl, she later moved to England where she married and had children; she died young of tuberculosis in 1943.

Until the outbreak of war, marriages were not uncommon between those who would later find themselves on opposing sides. That changed after hostilities began. The fervent patriotism that swept up volunteers into the regular armies and sent waves of war fever through civilian populations on all sides must surely have made citizens such as my great-aunt distinctly uncomfortable. Patriotic war fever was rife in Germany, as it was in England: from 1914 onwards Britons and other peoples from the United Kingdom who were living in Germany were arrested and interned in camps, principally Ruhleben in Berlin. Most of these were men; Lily would have been well aware of this. Many were sailors, arrested in the port of Hamburg and held in prison hulks on the river until they could be transferred to Berlin.[1] Anti-British and anti-French feelings were heated. I have no evidence that my great-aunt was incarcerated in Germany during this war, as was the case some twenty-three years later – ironically, in the very country of her birth. There were 1182 registered British subjects in Hamburg at the outbreak of war. In November 1914 – as the first numbers of men were arrested – women and children, and all of those over fifty years of age, were excluded. We can assume then, that Lily kept her freedom. It is hard to imagine that Lily did not experience hostility, or at least some form of isolation from those Hamburg citizens she had come to know – her German friends. She must have learned to live within a growing culture of anti-English sentiment. Lily and Carl were by now caught up in the emotional frenzy, beginning on 2 August 1914. Modris Eksteins writes of this time: 'the war has assumed the nature of a national, spiritual crusade, impossible to resist, uniting all Germans'; and he continues, 'In early August, Germans wallow in what appears to them a genuine synthesis of past and future, eternity embodied in the moment, and a resolution of all domestic strife – party versus party, class against class, sect against sect, church in conflict with state. Life has achieved transcendence.'[2]

This could not last. As the war dragged on, German casualties mounted: the wounded, the disfigured and the amputees were often reduced to begging on the street. How then could Lily not have come under pressure, as an enemy alien? By 1918 the war had reached the home front: starvation was common, and malnutrition was a certainty for most people. With its greater naval power and reach, England – Lily's home country – was blockading the German supply lines. The loss of morale, the hunger, the sheer war weariness led to a bitter climate of defeatism, with an increasing breakdown of the social contract.

The cheering crowds of 1914, waving their hats in packed public squares, were replaced by a growing atmosphere of anger and revolutionary ideas ranging from pacifism to communism. Not even the propaganda films churned out at Babelsberg (Germany's Hollywood), nor the appeals for war bonds, could stop the rot. In the final year of Germany's war with the Allies, secrecy, spying on each other with informers, all this must have made life even more intolerable. The armed forces were first in line for food; civilian hunger in 1916 had, by the following year, brought death by starvation – and riots over food.[3] Civilian conscription into armaments factories, especially of women (as with my grandmother Eunice in England), was one of many radical social changes. The hungry, malnourished workers toiled in dangerous conditions. This culture of total war throughout all combatant societies was a harbinger of worse to come from 1939 onwards.

Political extremism was the order of the day: the far-right parties and others fanning dissension and division, along with the rise of profiteering by those venal enough to take advantage. By the war's end, the Kaiser himself had become a marginal figure, sidelined by

The Munitions Girls, Stanhope Forbes, oil on canvas, 1918.
PUBLIC DOMAIN, LICENSED UNDER THE CREATIVE COMMONS
ATTRIBUTION ONLY LICENCE CC BY 4.0

Hindenburg and Ludendorff, the war generals. There arose among German civilians an increasing reaction to militarism, along with disillusion and cynicism on the frontlines. By January 1918 in Moabit Berlin, the central city, there were riots, and street battles between socialist speakers and their enemies. Strikers, their labour withheld as their only available weapon, were arrested and over 3000 were sent to the front. This was the world that Lily Hasenburg woke up to each morning: hungry, frightened, uncertain of the future, an alien citizen, sharing defeat with her host country that was unrecognisable from the confident Germany of the 1900s.

In building this picture of Lily's world, there were still profound gaps, personal and intimate. In the absence of letters and diaries, the alternative was to pursue her in any and every source of archival material, whatever the time and place. At home in Christchurch, I was picking up leftover traces from Berlin.

FIFTEEN

Great-uncle Uly and the Gestapo

Back on the trail of Lily and Carl, I was about to learn something that was hard to grasp at first: you often cannot find what you think you must have, only to discover there are many things you did not know you needed. On advice from the Red Cross, the next move was writing to the Swiss Embassy in Berlin, who kindly put me in touch with archivists in Bern. My letter follows.

26 January 2015

I am writing to ask for help and information about the repatriation of refugees and foreign nationals from Nazi Germany, through Switzerland in World War Two, especially in relation to the work of the Red Cross. My great-aunt Lilian Bywater was married to a German, Carl Hasenburg, a rubber trader from Hamburg. My great-uncle, her brother Ulysses Bywater, a former U.S. diplomat in Dresden, was able to have her repatriated to England with the intervention of the Red Cross.

The files of the Red Cross are presently closed to enquiries such as this, while they create and update a new database. My question concerns the availability of data and records from

Swiss official sources, about the identity of those people helped by the Red Cross, who came out of Germany and were repatriated via Switzerland. I do not have positive proof that she came out of Germany through your country, but it seems to me a good place to start and make an educated guess. I would be very grateful if you could help or advise me, who to contact in Switzerland.

I would be grateful for an email at least, as to where I can direct this enquiry.

Mit herzlichen Grüße ...

The answers were not long in coming: the archivists in Bern went to work and soon forwarded to me all that they could find on the name Bywater from that period. This proved to be a goldmine: files arrived – photocopies of material my great-uncle Uly had written for the French and German newspapers on his travels as a journalist in January 1940 through Nazi Germany, at war with Britain and France before the May Blitzkrieg. These files included reports for the newspapers *Paris-soir* and *Weltwoche*, written by Uly from Germany in February 1940.[1] He had travelled on his American passport, based on his bogus identity as one New York-born. He wrote accounts of the German citizens he had talked to, including a top Luftwaffe general, Ernst Udet, First World War fighter ace, an extrovert who was never shy of seeking notice. They met in the swanky Hotel Adlon in Berlin: that's the kind of chutzpah this uncle of mine had.

Uly writes more on his adventures: he describes his return to Bern after being strip-searched by the Gestapo at the border, as a man by then well into his fifties. At the start of the *Paris-soir* article, he makes a point of stating he has a relative in Germany (no name is given, but we know it was Lily). It is more than likely he either met up with her at the time, or made contact with her in Hamburg, where she was living alone without her husband. Carl Hasenburg, who was in England at the outbreak of the war, had been picked up in a swoop on German nationals and interned in Seaton Camp, Devon. He was later sent by ship to spend the next five years in Canadian internment camps, and survived the conflict. He was fortunate not to have been

Adlon Hotel, Berlin, April 1945. PHOTO 12/ALAMY STOCK PHOTO

on an earlier shipment carrying internees, which was torpedoed by U-boats and sunk with great loss of life. We now know how and why Carl Hasenburg survived the war, safe in Canada; he returned to the United Kingdom in 1945 and was later repatriated to Germany.[2]

What follows is Uly's account of his trip to Berlin from Bern in late December 1939 and early January 1940, before the Blitzkrieg and the invasion of the Low Countries and France in May. He was travelling on a US passport. This extract, taken from *Weltwoche*, 1940, has been translated from the original German.[3]

Eindrucke von einer Reise durchs Dritte Reich
(Impressions of a journey through the Third Reich)

Today, we continue the series of articles begun yesterday, which are the story of a recent trip to Germany. The author is a neutral observer who has long lived in the Reich, and he still has family there, which prevents him revealing her name.[4] *We know from impartial testimony about living life in the Third Reich after four months of war, this is appearing – the same time as in* Paris-soir *– in major newspapers of neutral or belligerent countries.*

I arrived in Berlin on the night of St. Silvestre (December 31st). The station at Friedrichstraße was plunged into total darkness. There was a porter on the platform, my train arrived in the station with a five and a half hour delay. For my fellow passengers, a delay of five and a half hours on a journey of fourteen hours was quite normal.

Each day raises questions about the situation in the Third Reich. One would like to know what it looks like, how much the Germans have to eat, how they live and whether Nazism is about to collapse. That's why I went to Germany, to answer these questions for myself. And I succeeded. The truth is, as you will see from my reports, different in many ways from the stories that are told abroad about the Third Reich.

The weeks that I was in Germany – spent traveling from west to east, from north to south, from Frankfurt to Danzig, from Stettin to Dresden, Berlin and Munich – were interesting, if not always very pleasant. I ate precious little bread and virtually no butter. So today I weigh two and a half kilos less than before my entry into the Third Reich. I spoke in the Adlon Bar in Berlin with Ernst Udet, Goering's right hand man. I traveled on the often really unsatisfactory railways by first, second and third class. I frequently began long conversations with my fellow passengers, often remaining silent in order to be better able to hear what they had to say. I met people of all kinds: bank directors, soldiers, airmen, taxi drivers, housewives, shopkeepers and waiters. I also talked with neutral diplomats and kept my eyes open.

I was even temporarily observed by the Gestapo, whose agents took few pains to hide their activity. For a while they followed me whenever I left the hotel. They walked a few steps behind me, stopped when I stopped, moved when I kept moving and in the beer halls they sat down at the table next to mine. I could only escape them when I took a taxi; because today only a quarter of the taxis are in operation, it means that no more than one is free at a time, so that there was no car left for the agent to follow me. I have been able to visit many people in this way. Nevertheless, I found myself frightened when I crossed over the border at my departure. Customs officers in their green uniforms had searched all my luggage, all I possessed was emptied out. Even the covering of my suitcase was searched, only then did the officers make the 'cleared' chalk mark on it.

'Finished?' I enquired. 'Yes,' he replied. 'Then I will go and have a glass of beer until it's time for my train.' He nodded and I walked away, but I did not get far. A hand was laid on my shoulder, a field gray SS officer said, 'Please for a moment, come with me.' Then he led me into a not too narrow cell, 'Take it off,' he said, pointing at my coat. I obeyed. 'Take it all off,' he said, pointing at my trousers.

'Everything? Shall I be naked in front of you?', I asked. 'Yes!' But even when I was standing stark naked in front of him, the official was still not satisfied. He felt between my toes, told me to open my mouth and looked inside. Then he took all my clothes away behind a folding screen and one could hear a buzzing noise. 'For heaven's sake,' I cried out, 'what are you doing? That's my only suit!'

'He is elderly,' declared a voice through the curtain. My suit was actually being scanned with X-rays, piece by piece, underpants and socks, shoes and all, to discover whether or not something secret was hidden there. Fortunately, my thoughts could not be discovered with X-rays. An hour and a half later, finally back in a neutral country, I ate the first fresh egg I'd tasted for three weeks.[5]

What follows is a transcription of a Swiss police report on my great-uncle's activities in his accommodation in Bern, which rendered him a suspicious person in that wartime culture.

Swiss Police Report, 18 February 1940

End of January 1940 it was notified to the ND Security and Criminal Police of the City of Bern:

> 'Bywater Ulysses, born 08/02/1880, Hotel Gotthard in Bern, was suspicious because he telephones all the time. He must be a real snooper: economies always come into the conversation.'

The person in question is identified as:

> 'Bywater Ulysses, of Peter and Marie née Summer, citizen of the USA, born 02/08/80 in Rockferry, banker, was last resident in the Hotel Gotthard in Bern.'

This will be according to his information in the city. Immigration police have earlier already variously detained (him) in Switzerland; among other things, he also, at the end of December 1939, for the purpose of transit to Danzig, possessed a visa for five days.[6]

On 6.1.40 he came in Bern recently to the police, allegedly for registration in preparation for departure and stayed at the Hotel Gotthard. The police of Canton Bern issued him a residence permit to 15.02.40 and on 14/02/40, he traveled to Paris.

As already mentioned, Bywater has acted suspiciously in restaurants, that he was interested in all possibilities. However, no concrete case can be brought where it is known that it had been to do with matters in the context of our national defence.

At the hotel he has received no visits and his phone calls were only in connection with American Express; he has not received

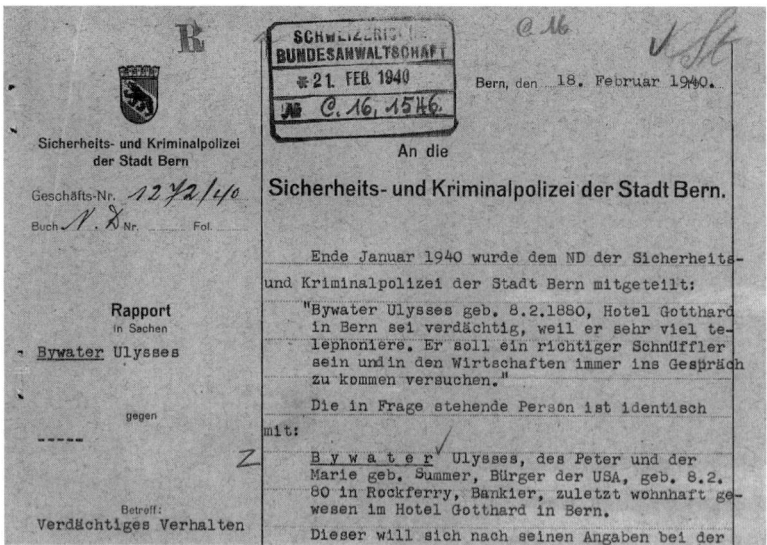

Scan of Swiss police report: Uly is deemed 'Ein richtiger Schnüffler', 'a right snooper' – a sleuth. IMAGE SUPPLIED BY SWISS GOVERNMENT ARCHIVES, BERN

a large amount of correspondence. After his conversation in the hotel, he could have applied mainly for a visa for France and England; the latter has been denied him, allegedly because he had just previously been residing in Germany.

He has had conversations with a city official. Immigration police tell of his experiences during his trip to Germany and from these accounts, it appears then that Bywater is almost certainly the author of several articles in *Paris-soir* and probably also of those in the *Weltwoche*, since in the two newspapers, one speaks of (him) being with the Air Force General Udet in the Adlon-Bar in Berlin. Regarding the allegation of the official concerned, Bywater was at least the author of the articles in *Paris-soir*. The clippings of the articles concerned follow here as appendices.

Something suspicious here appears: Bywater before his departure for Germany has asserted in insulting ways about the Third

Reich and then has journeyed backwards and forwards there. These circumstances could cause him to appear in the light of an Agent Provocateur, but concrete evidence, one way or another, of illegal activities did not present itself.

However, if Bywater is indeed the author of the article in *Weltwoche*, this could be an offence against the Alien Policing Rules, since he was prohibited from taking any gainful employment.[7]

Sighted: 19 Feb. 1940 Criminal Commissioner.
Signed xx
Security and Criminal Police/ News Agency
Signed xx
At The Swiss Attorney General, Bern, City Police Director.
Signed xx

So what does all this mean? To have sprung Lily, in the year before she appears in England, Ulysses Bywater needed help. Intuition suggests to me that, when he met Ernst Udet, the First World War ace and senior Luftwaffe official, in the Hotel Adlon in early January 1940, he raised the matter of his sister's desire to return to England, and explained that her husband was now dead. In a *Paris-soir* article on his time in Germany in January 1940 (where he meets Udet), he begins his claim to an insider's knowledge, mentioning his former long residence in Germany where he still has family, 'which prevents me from revealing her name'.[8] He writes of a long drinking session with the German leader, the best of champagne ordered by his host. We know that Udet, at this stage in his career, is feeling badly disaffected with his position in the Luftwaffe, and with Hermann Göring's refusal to take him seriously (both men were former fighter aces). Udet was a known bon vivant, with a love for meeting and impressing foreigners; drinking and dining with an American journalist from a French newspaper, when your country is at war with France, tells us something.[9] Uly also had his own family to help him; his son John was working as an

Ernst Udet (left) and Hermann Göring, 1941. SUEDDEUTSCHE ZEITUNG PHOTO/ALAMY STOCK PHOTO

American diplomat in the Swiss Embassy in Bern. John would have had both motivation and means to help in getting his aunt Lily out of Hamburg, into Bern, and sanctuary.

Here is my hunch: Uly made up the story of 'a murdered Jewish husband' to get Lily out of Germany, via Switzerland, sometime in mid to late 1940. This is what he tells his nephew Robin, and what Robin later tells me. Why would Ulysses lie to his nephew? To keep things consistent: after all, he has just got his sister out of Germany and into England, with a lie.

However it happened, whatever was said, Lily Hasenburg left Hamburg just in time. She escaped from a city that was bombed by the RAF in late July–early August 1943 in Operation Gomorrah, the Hamburg Firestorm. The English writer Stephen Spender, who visited Hamburg in 1945, wrote:

15: Great-uncle Uly and the Gestapo

Hamburg in ruins after Operation Gomorrah, 24–30 July 1943.
SUEDDEUTSCHE ZEITUNG PHOTO/ALAMY STOCK PHOTO

> This is Hamburg as I saw it in August 1945. All legends of the living city have been superseded by the legend of the dead one. In a great air raid, when fire bombs were dropped in a ring around the centre of the city, the immense heat of the fire caused a whirlwind in which flames rushed from building to building, and thousands of people were roasted alive.[10]

If Carl and Lily had not been interned, what might their fate have been, in the firestorm that consumed Klosterallee 20?

SIXTEEN

Lily is Interned on the Isle of Man

WHAT, THEN, OF ULY'S NEPHEW ROBIN'S CLAIM THAT THE Red Cross were somehow involved? So far, the Red Cross have been unable to provide me with any details of this – as we have seen in Robin Bywater's 1990 letter to me – but there is documentary proof from the Swiss archives of Lily's arrival in England, early in 1941. She was locked up in Holloway Prison with other 'enemy aliens'.[1] These were German women, many of them Jewish refugees. The Swiss archives provided me with correspondence from London in 1941 that showed which of the German internees on the Isle of Man had accepted a form of support. They had turned up correspondence between J.J. Huber of the Swiss Legation in London and Commander Joanna Cruickshank at the Rushen Women's Internment Camp on the Isle of Man in December 1940. Payment was made to the internees, from the Nazi regime in Germany. This 'Taschengeld' (pocket money) had come from 'the German Reich'. Lily Hasenburg was one of a number of women who accepted this money (many Jewish women had refused).

A Home Office letter on this matter dated 4 August 1941, sent to the Swiss Legation in London, states: 'the accompanying list ... gives the names of 347 women in the Women's Internment Camp *who profess allegiance to the Reich and who are willing to accept payment from the German Government*'.[2] The letter mentioned that this money was 'additional to the payment of £1, which is to be made to those women [interned since] March 31st'.[3] A copy of Commander Cruickshank's reply was attached. The next letter on this matter, from the Home Office in Bournemouth on 4 August 1941 to the same J.J. Huber, gives the names of those women. On page 6 of this list we read, '272. HASSENBURG Lilian-Edith'. Her name is misspelt, but this is certainly my great-aunt. This is the closest we may come to her conflicted loyalties; at least we now know she was back in England by then – if not exactly when she left Germany behind. Eighteen months after her brother Uly's meeting with Udet in Berlin, Lily is now safe in England. Another list attached, from Holloway Prison, London, in March 1940, contains a similar group of twenty-seven women internees who agreed to receive the £1; and 45 'Who do NOT wish to receive £1.0.0.' I'm led to conclude that those refusing are in all likelihood Jewish refugees, fleeing their German homes, and refusing blood money from the Nazi regime.

While we may not know quite how Lily came from Germany to England in 1940–41, we see from the above, and from the evidence following, that by early in 1941 she was interned on the Isle of Man. On the advice of my bookseller friend at the National Archives in London, I contacted Alan Franklin, the librarian at Manx National Heritage Library at the Manx Museum. Did they have any records pertaining to Lily Hasenburg? His reply was swift, and apologetic; there were 'only partial records for her, as pasted below' – but what records they were! From no documentary evidence at all, here was a transcript from the Isle of Man Constabulary police record of female internees. The information given relates to three different matters: her appeal for release in 1941, which was declined; her release on compassionate grounds to visit her gravely ill daughter Anita in Liverpool in 1943; and a reference to her status later that year, on the Rushen Women's Camp rolls.[4]

Hasenburg Lilian Edith
Rushen Camp, Port Erin. – Date of Birth 18.8.1876 in London. – Police Permit to proceed out of Rushen Internment Camp under escort for the purpose of appearing before the Home Office Advisory Committee at the Court House, Douglas, on Wednesday 26th March 1941, at 9.45 a.m.

(Box IOMC Movement Permits) – Was given temporary release from 9th to the 17th April 1943 for the purpose of proceeding to Liverpool to visit her daughter who was ill in hospital. She was not due back until the 27th, but when in Liverpool she received a letter from the Home Office informing her that she must return to the Isle of Man on the 24th. This she did but without a permit. She arrived at the Camp and it was later confirmed that whilst on the train from Douglas to Port Erin she was not asked to show a permit.

Temp Folder18Z5-9-47 TO. –
Still in 'W' Camp 25.10.1943. – From MNHL MS 11551/5 (TNA HO 215/478) Women's Camp Nominal Rolls.

Alan Franklin's letter had this to add:

> You will see the date of birth is in fact a year earlier than you thought; this information is mainly extracted from the IOM Police records that we hold (they administered the Internees), and also a camp nominal roll held by the National Archives in London. She was on the island for at least two years 1941–1943 and appeared before a review tribunal in 1941 to plead for release, which I assume, must have been rejected. We have no record of when she was eventually released, she would have been one of the oldest internees as in her sixties, but all ages were held in the camp.

I had also supplied Alan with names of those German women I had discovered that Lily was living with in Islington N16 after the war ended. He wrote back that they had not been internees on the island, but he speculated 'that it was a refugee house [and] she might perhaps have been a supervisor due to her age?'

By far the most important details are contained in the dates of her permission to visit 'her daughter who was ill in hospital'. I knew there must be a connection with Anita's death in 1943. A date in the record seemed familiar to me: I had seen it on the family gravestone in Allerton Cemetery Liverpool when I visited in October 2013. Searching my photographs from there, I found her date of death: 10 April 1943.[5]

A few days later, Anita Fincken's death certificate arrived (I had ordered it earlier): it gave the cause of death as pulmonary tuberculosis. If Lily had managed to take a ferry and a train on her release day from Rushen Camp – which is not a certainty – she may just have reached her daughter on her deathbed. As it was, she stayed for the funeral. Her early recall to Rushen, with or without a permit, was one more twist of the knife. Anita's death at the young age of thirty-three, from what we would now call a disease of poverty, does raise more questions. What was the history of this ailment in her life? It is now well known that malnutrition impairs our immunity and so predisposes us to tuberculosis, when exposed; while tuberculosis itself is a known cause of malnutrition: once contracted, it remains in the system and further stress (such as poor diet and a recurrence of malnutrition) could certainly cause a fatal relapse.

Did the hunger years of Anita's childhood in Germany during the Great War, when Germans starved en masse due to the Allied blockade, create the conditions for her to contract the disease? Did Britain's wartime rationing from 1939 onwards weaken her resistance and lead to a relapse? All of this was entirely possible. There is nothing more recorded at my disposal in my lean family history from this period, but we can imagine the sorrow felt by her mother, her husband, her daughter, her aunt (my grandmother), and by her cousin (my mother) as well. All this in the midst of a war consuming the world in that same grief. As for Aunt Lily, we know that she left the Isle of Man at the end of the war; very likely, not before the

Bywater family grave, Allerton Cemetery, Liverpool: Anita Fincken, 10 April 1943.

German surrender in May 1945. After burying Anita, her grieving mother was now facing two more years in the camp; there is no record of an earlier release.

When she appears again on the written record, in London in 1946, she is seventy years old; one of scores of women who populated the postwar world, bereft of husbands, brothers, sisters, children. She, of course, had a husband – perhaps estranged, but a husband alive; and she still had a brother, a sister and a son. When Anita died in 1943, it is fair to assume that Lily stayed in Liverpool with her sister, my grandmother Eunice. Her home at 17 Hunters Lane, Wavertree, was less than half an hour's walk from Anita's residence at 1 Colindale Road, Childwall. Perhaps it was my grandmother – and Anita's husband Christopher – who added Anita's name to the tombstone, alongside that of Nanny's daughter Lillian, my aunt, and those of my great-grandparents. That same year, Nanny Eunice left for London, following her daughter (my mother) and her sailor husband, all leaving Liverpool behind. My grandmother never spoke of her sister being in London after the war – only of her death. Lily's son Carl and his wife Irma lived nearby in London. Would Lily return to a broken, defeated Germany, now that her sister, her brother, her son and his wife, fellow survivors, were all in London?

Alan Franklin from the Isle of Man gets back in touch, sending links to the Manx National Heritage Museum website with details of a book, *Living with the Wire*. Edited by Yvonne Cresswell, it was published in conjunction with a 1994 exhibition on the island. Growing interest since, sparked by the Isle of Man featuring in the BBC TV genealogy show, *Who Do You Think You Are?*, led to the book being republished in 2010. Former internees, civilian staff, military personnel and their families contributed stories, photographs, pictures, postcards, paintings and handmade items, along with official documentation from both wars. The greatest enemy in the camps was boredom. Internees in the Great War and in the Second World War set about creating an active culture of education, music, drama, arts and crafts, sport, all manner of productive diversions – as well as cooking, cleaning and generally managing their own affairs, within the wire. In Lily's case, from 1941 onwards she was interned in the women's camp at Rushen, on the southernmost tip of the island near Port Erin and Port St Mary. Something of her life there, until her release, is made clear from rich contributions by the other inhabitants at Rushen Camp that appear in the book.

Opened on 30 May 1940, Rushen was unlike the other camps: it consisted of a series of billets with local families who were paid a guinea a week by the Home Office authorities, who had charge of the women (the men were supervised by the military). The women were not confined behind the wire: they had access to the beaches, which was a boon especially to those with young children. Visits were arranged for husbands and wives who were separated, and a special camp was later set up for married couples. There were lectures, and classes to improve English language skills. Lily might well have taken part in these: she must have been a German speaker to some degree, after forty years of marriage to Carl, living in Hamburg. She may even have been involved in teaching English to German detainees. Former residents have spoken of the kindness of most people on the Isle of Man, especially in Port Erin, where 4000 internees were shoehorned in among the local population until the camp ceased operation in September 1945. Lily was then moved to her address in London – as noted earlier – where she was housed with German refugees at 177 Green Lanes, Islington N16.

What today may seem an unfair deprivation of liberty (my great-aunt was still a British citizen) can also be viewed as a series of fortunate events. Had she remained in Germany, the pressure on Lily as war came home to the Germans would have only become more intense. The Allied bombing campaign – such as the Hamburg firestorm in 1943, described earlier – the battles to liberate Europe and defeat Hitler, saw her fellow citizens reap the misery they had sown among conquered peoples from 1939 onwards. She may very likely not have survived. Whatever the circumstances of her leaving Germany, her internment on the Isle of Man meant that she was safely in Rushen, where there were none of the perils of living in Liverpool or London. She did not have to deal with the German bombing campaigns and, later, the terrifying V-weapon attacks her sister (my grandmother) endured and survived – along with my mother, my father's family, and millions of others in England. This says nothing about her inner life: her grief and loneliness can easily be imagined. Compared to countless other civilians on all sides of this conflict, however, we might fairly say that from 1941 onwards at least, my great-aunt Lily Hasenburg lived a very fortunate war.

There is also some documentary evidence of her involvement during the war, in 1943, on behalf of her husband (which suggests they were in contact, while interned separately). Enquiries in 2015 with the International Committee of the Red Cross (ICRC), through the New Zealand Red Cross Family Tracing Service, proved most helpful.[6] Lily was visited by the ICRC in July 1943; their report on the meeting reads: 'Karl is an internee at Camp 31 in Canada.

He complains about the poor unhealthy housing conditions and the fact that he is only allowed to stay in the open air for one hour a day. Mrs Hasenburg asks if the C.O.C.R. delegate in Canada can intervene and requests, for reasons of age and health, his transfer to Camp No. 42.' With Lily pursuing this matter on her husband's behalf, this late in the war, he certainly does not resemble the 'Jewish husband killed by the Nazis' from the story told me by Lily's nephew Robin in 1990.

There is no more information than this on the document, but another file on Carl Hasenburg from the same source tells us more. Among other things, we learn that Carl's address at the time of his arrest in February 1940 was 14 Canning Street, Liverpool. So at the same time as Lily's brother Uly is travelling in Germany and visiting her in Hamburg, Carl is residing in Liverpool: his occupation is listed as 'Previously rubber merchant (merchant navy)'. At the age of sixty-six, with no previous marine history, it is difficult to believe he was ever a sailor. From the document, we learn more of Carl's history:

> Civilian internee ... Seaton Camp, Devon ... 05.02.1940 ...
> Interned in Canada, Camp 'R' ... list 27.03.1941 ...
> Interned in Camp 31, Fort Henry, Canada ... 13.08.1943 ...
> Transferred from Camp 31 ... to Camp 22, Canada ... 19.01.1944 ...
> Returned to the United Kingdom on 18.05.1945 [according to a list dated 16.11.1945]

All of these events are attested by the British authorities and the ICRC, from the list sent by their delegation in Canada. This was news to me: that Carl was not only arrested and interned in England (which we knew), but that he was living and working there, in Canning Street, Liverpool, a short ten-minute drive (today) from my Nanny's home in Hunters Lane. This tells me that my mother must have met him, as she was living at home at that time. She never said so, nor did my grandmother ever reveal that she had seen him again, so long after having his child – but it's difficult to believe there was no contact. The deeper

I go into this labyrinth, the more light – the more darkness. I was not sure if Carl or Lily ever saw each other in England at the end of the war, or what might have happened; all I could do was to keep looking for clues.

The search seemed to have gone cold again. I was checking now and then on Ancestry.com, to see if more hints had surfaced. Having had my enthusiasm renewed by a search on a Jewish ancestry website, given to me by Leonie Wiemeyer, a German contact, I searched again for Hasenburg/berg – and then at last, results! 'Lilian E. Hassenburg' began showing up on postwar North London electoral rolls, in the Borough of Islington. There she was, living in London in 1946, 1947 (my birth year) and 1948 – when the entries stopped. In the final entry, Lily resides at 177 Green Lanes Islington N16, a three-storey semi-detached residence, with seven other women, all with German names, in the same building: Becker, Laumer, Neubert, Pahl, Reske, Scheiterlein and Wolfarht. Could this be a group of women released from internment on the Isle of Man? Alan Franklin, the librarian at Manx National Heritage Library, told me later that these names were not those of women who had been in Rushen Camp, but they were possibly other refugees, among hundreds of thousands of displaced persons in the United Kingdom, with millions in Germany and all the rest of Europe.

How close we had come, back then! In my first year on the planet, I was living and breathing a mere 15 miles from Great-aunt Lily. I was cuddled by her sister, my Nanny Eunice; she knew where Lily was, surely, and she would have seen her often in those postwar years? I'll never know if Great-aunt Lily laid eyes on me.

This was hair-prickling stuff and material to revisit. The next question was, where did she go after 1948? Did she die from cancer at that time, as my grandmother had told me? An email to the Islington Borough Council yielded no answer, but it gave me a link to the local cemeteries. A search for her on Deceased Online, a database of UK burial and cremation records, yields, not Lily, but her son Carl and his wife Irma. With this information, I discover they were cremated, and I can visit to pay my respects at Kensal Green Cemetery, Ashes Plot

62579/224/64. There is now somewhere to go, to follow the mystery of Carl – of Pip – to whatever these graves will tell me. Still a long way from information about their lives – from a story that might reward me with human details – but it represents a small victory.

Did Lily go back to Germany after 1948? That's possible – so is it likely? If not, she must have died in England, perhaps even having changed her German married name back to Bywater. More searches don't help me in this. Is she in England somewhere, and is there more of her story between 1943 and 1948 where, so far, any evidence is missing? History beckons, challenges me, whispering, 'Come closer: I may be the Past ... but who are you?'

SEVENTEEN

Looking into the Graves

O N MANUEL'S ADVICE, I HAVE WRITTEN TO THE CHURCH Archives in Radevormwald – Carl's birthplace – to see what we can discover about his religious affiliations, and also to the City Archives of Wuppertal, the nearest urban centre. Heinz Dietsch of the Radevormwald church is not long in responding and his email is not encouraging: 'Unfortunately there are no church records for the period (1874). All of the church books of the Lutheran congregation 1810–1935 were lost by 1945 in the war'. Manuel, informed of this, is still hopeful we will get a reply from Wuppertal soon, and that might give us Carl's profession. We need to try and find the parish and the cemetery; but he also warns me that unless some family members have been paying the lease, 'graves in Germany don't normally exist forever'. I wonder what happens when that occurs, as there must be many times when this is the case. Our system here, where we buy a plot in perpetuity – barring erosion, earthquakes, grave robbers, motorway extensions and other disturbers of the dead – is much kinder.

He agrees with me that placing an advertisement in a local newspaper, or even ringing a random Hasenburg in the Radevormwald or Önkfeld area, might be a way forward, as some certainly still live there. I don't have long to wait before more riches arrive: a few days later, details from the death register in the Wuppertal city archive come by letter. At last, I can see what happened to my great-aunt Lily after 1948, when she was last heard of living in Islington N16. Carl Hasenburg's death certificate is rich in detail concerning him, but it also reveals this: 'Der Verstorbene war verheiratet mit der bereits verstorbenen Lilian Edith Hasenburg geboren Bywater, zuletzt wohnhaft in Hagen' (The deceased was married to Lilian Edith Hasenburg, née Bywater who predeceased him and formerly lived in Hagen).

We have found her! Lily, you did move back to Germany, as I suspected. She was living in the city of Hagen near Wuppertal when she died, sometime between 1948 and 1954 – the same city that is given as Carl's last address: Hagen, Körnerstraße 94. Were they back together? At last, something concrete to deal with: we now have a line between birth and death, for them both. There is much more: as well as the names of his parents who appeared on the birth certificate, there is also Carl's profession, the name of the informant who identified him, the cause of death, the place, and the time of death. Carl Hasenburg in his seventy-ninth year was identified as a Lutheran who lived in Hagen at the above address, where he had been, at some time, a 'Privat-Sprachlehrer' – a private language teacher (I'm guessing, of English, given his association with England and his English wife). He died at 6.45pm on 9 May 1954 in Wuppertal, at Kurvenstraße 48, the home of Emmy Böhmer, a seamstress, who identified him for the purposes of this register. Either he was visiting or he was living there at the time; he died of cancer, so it is unlikely to have been a sudden death. It is all at once overwhelming: I do not know what to feel.

We now have a whole new field to explore. How did Lily come to be back in Carl's life, and when did she die? Who was Emmy Böhmer? What are the Hasenburg family connections from this time, that might still provide a clue as to his early life? Love is strange, but one thing does make a kind of sense: if Lily had finally broken up with Carl, he does have a record as a philanderer, in my mother's account of his dalliance with my grandmother Eunice. I need to follow her back into Germany and see if there are any family connections to

Carl in his home area. Acting on a suggestion from Manuel, I make an online search for newspapers in the Wuppertal–Hagen area and come up with the *Westdeutsche Zeitung*. With my limited German, scrolling through the various links leads me to a list of reporters. Here is another Manuel to help me: Manuel Praest (am I in Spain here, I wonder?).

I compose a request and, in a day or two, Wuppertal Manuel replies that he is willing to help. Manuel in Hamburg, once more to the rescue, sends me a short plea for information composed and ready:

> Dr. Jeffrey Paparoa Holman, Schriftsteller und Historiker aus Christchurch in Neuseeland, bittet um Hilfe bei der Suche nach Informationen über seine Großtante, deren Mann aus der Gegend um Wuppertal stammte. Er schreibt: 'Meine englische Großtante Lilian Edith Bywater heiratete 1898 in Liverpool, Carl Hasenburg. Er ist 1874 in Önkfeld geboren und 1954 in Wuppertal gestorben. Zuvor lebte er in Hagen; meine Großtante, die vor ihm verstarb, lebte ebenfalls dort. Ich hoffe auf Kontakt von Verwandten der Hasenburgs, die mir mit Informationen über Carl und seine Frau helfen können.'
>
> Dr. Holman kann unter folgender E-Mail-Adresse erreicht werden ...[1]

For several days I hear nothing (nor does Wuppertal Manuel acknowledge receipt of this – he is, after all, a busy journalist). Then suddenly, after Easter, a burst of three email replies arrive in my inbox: Roland, who knew a Hasenburg from school days in the 1950s and gives me his friend's address; Rainer, whose grandparents had lived in an apartment from 1916 onwards with one Hermann Hasenburg and his wife – he remembered them as a child; and the most likely candidate, one Klaus Niepman, whose mother was a Hasenburg from the Önkfeld–Radevormwald area. All offer to help me further if they can, so I reply to each of them and wait. It often occurs to me in this process that family history searches are a waiting game, full of sudden surprises that lighten long stretches of silence and uncertainty.

In the meantime, my Hamburg Manuel has written to the authorities in Hagen, as we now know that Lily died there, but not when. In April, a reply from Andreas Korthals, an archivist at Stadtarchiv Hagen, advises me that the records for Lily's death exist and if I remit 18 euro, they will send me a copy. Organising bank transfers complicates the process but finally, in late May 2015, proof arrives of the last day of Lily's turbulent life. She died at 1.45am on 27 January 1951 in the Evangelischen Krankenhaus (Protestant Hospital) at Hagen: the cause of death is given as uterine cancer. Her address is the same as on Carl's death certificate three years later; it is not he who identifies her, however, but a hospital administrator. I really don't know what to feel, reading this: so much more than I knew before, but still, so little, so bare. I want to go there, to find the place where she lived, and where she was buried, even if the grave no longer exists; to get as close as I can to where my grandmother's sister took her last breath. Although it seems we never met, we are flesh and blood, bone on bone. That's how it is and how it always will be.

I don't have long to wait for the next piece of news. An email arrives from Manuel in Hamburg:

> Dear Jeffrey, again I have to bring you bad news: It seems that the graves of Carl and Lilian don't exist anymore. I sent an enquiry to the cemetery office and to the Stadtarchiv in Hagen, but they can't find anything in their files. I recommend that we make an enquiry to the parish office in Hagen to get information about the burials. I can write a letter in the course of this week. At least we will know if they were buried in Hagen. Warm greetings, Manuel.

There it is: no grave to visit, no material marker of these elusive lives. This feeling – I cannot go and stand before the place where their last remains lie – is like another, small death. The question of why their graves no longer exist and what happens when a grave is reused will have to wait. In the meantime, there is hope that Manuel can access church records, so we can at least see where they were buried sixty long years ago.

I am left wondering: did her son Carl junior, living in London, attend his mother's funeral in Hagen? His father Carl was still alive; wouldn't he have been in touch with their son? When my grandmother, her sister Eunice, came to live with us in New Zealand later in 1951, she must have known of her sister's death. Their brother Uly, too, did he go to her funeral? They would have been in contact when their sister died, surely? It seems certain they all saw each other, more than once, while Lily lived in London from 1945 till 1948. They had all survived five years of total war. What chance? My Nanny was certainly in contact with Carl and Irma – Lily's son and daughter-in-law. She had the address of her surrogate 'lost boy' Carl, in that old address book we have encountered before in this journey. I pick it up now, opening it one more time at 'H' for Hasenburg. There, in my grandmother's hand, in the 1930s to the 1960s, are the ghostly fingerprints of the lost.

This all takes me some time to absorb; to be honest, I feel deflated, if not defeated. There is nowhere to go and mourn. I can only think of what life in Nazi Germany was like for Lily, exposed, as were all the other Germans around her, to the poison of the Hitler years. What influence did the rise of Nazi culture in the wider historic German world have on Lily's making that remark about Hitler in 1934? I think of her life during and after the Great War in Germany in 1918, a people starving and the country wracked by civil war. As Julia Boyd writes, 'there was really only one issue that mattered to Berliners in 1919, and that was food'.[2] Worse was to come: hyperinflation, peaking in 1923, all but destroyed the middle classes: 'many were in total penury ... having sold their last possessions ... many of them, doctors, lawyers, teachers, preferred to swallow poison rather than suffer the shame of starvation'.[3] Germany recovered slowly in the Weimar years, 1924–29, but worse was to come. The poet Stephen Spender, visiting Hamburg in the late 1920s, wrote of what he saw there – even before the 1929 crash on Black Thursday, 24 October – of being 'oppressed by the poverty' he had seen in Hamburg the previous summer. He observed how 'prostitutes could be regarded as merchandise'; but now, 'as carrion'.[4] He wrote of 'the folk story of the workless wanderers in the Germany of 1929 ... a saga of all this German youth which had been born into war, starved in the blockade, stripped in the inflation – [who] now, with no money and no beliefs ... sprang like a breed of dragon's teeth waiting for its leader, into the centre of Europe'.[5] It was as if the postwar political chaos and economic hardship of the previous decade were now to be revisited on the German people, with a vengeance.

German activist and writer Simone Weil, on a visit from Paris to Berlin to report on the situation for her trade union newspaper, wrote that in 1932, with the nation still on its knees, 'everyone who has pinned all his hopes on the victory of the working class ... ought right now to have his eyes on Germany'.[6] In *The Visionaries*, Wolfram Eilenberger writes of this moment: 'What [Weil] saw on the ground in Berlin was a nation on its knees.'[7] Her comments echo and reinforce Spender's observations. 'In Germany,' she writes, 'you see former engineers who manage to eat one cold meal a day by renting chairs in the public gardens; you see elderly men in stiff collars and bowler hats begging at subway exits or singing in cracked voices in the streets. Students are dropping out of school and selling peanuts, matches or shoelaces on the street ... Every worker expects some time or other to be thrown into compulsory idleness that is the lot of *nearly half of the German working class*.'[8]

We can imagine Lily and Carl's struggles. His business had long gone bust: there were no takers, it seems. With Hitler soon to be seen as saviour – Germany would go on to recover, as the Nazis militarised the economy in the mid 1930s – it is not so difficult to understand Lily's embrace of the Führer, along with hundreds and thousands of other Germans. Dear Lily, my long-lost great-aunt, where to now? Liebe Lily, meine lange velorene Tante, wohin jetzt, wohin?

> Lilian Edith Hasenburg, born Bywater, England, living in Hagen, Körnerstraße 94, died on 27 January 1951, at 1.45am, at the Protestant Hospital.
> The deceased was born on 18 August 1876 in London (England), registry unknown.

Both parents, unknown. The deceased was married to Karl Hasenburg.
Death registered at the hospital (signed). Age: 75.
Cause of death: Uterine cancer. The deceased married on 23.6.1898, in Liverpool.[9]

Carl Hasenburg, Private Language Teacher, Protestant, residing in Hagen, Körnerstraße 94, has died on 9 May 1954, at 1845 hours, in Wuppertal, Kurvenstraße 48.
The deceased was born on 15 September 1874 in Radevormald, Nr 242.
His father, Carl Hasenburg last resided in Radevormald.
His mother, Emma Caroline Hasenburg, born Höller, formerly resided in Turse, Kreis Dirschau.
The deceased, predeceased by Lilian Edith Hasenburg, born Bywater, last resided in Hagen.
Witnessed by Emily Böhmer, Master seamstress from the same address.
She identified herself by her ID card and declares that she learned of this death through her own knowledge.
Cause of death: Wasting Cancer. Emaciation (cachexia)
Marriage: 23.6.1898. Liverpool.[10]

Opposite: Lily Hasenburg's death certificate, Hagen, Germany, 27 January 1951. ARCHIVES, STADT-HAGEN

Nr. 36   C

                          Hagen, den 27. Januar 19 51

Die Lilian Edith Hasenburg, geborene Bijwater
                              evangelisch

wohnhaft in Hagen, Körnerstraße 94
ist am 27. Januar 1951 um 1 Uhr 45 Minuten
in Hagen, im evangelischen Krankenhause verstorben.
Die Verstorbene war geboren am 18. August 1876
in London (England)
(Standesamt unbekannt   Nr. unbekannt)
Vater: unbekannt

Mutter: unbekannt

Die Verstorbene war — ~~nicht~~ — verheiratet mit Karl Hasenburg.

Eingetragen auf ~~mündliche~~ — schriftliche — Anzeige der Verwaltung
des Krankenhauses.
~~Der Anzeigende~~

~~Vorgelesen, genehmigt und unterschrieben~~

                              Der Standesbeamte
                              [signature]

Todesursache: Gebärmutterkrebs.

Eheschließung der Verstorbenen am 23.6.1898 in Liverpool
(Standesamt Liverpool (England)   Nr. unbekannt).

EIGHTEEN

From the Hotel Adlon to Kensal Green

In July of 2015 there's a chance to return to England and Germany; Jeanette has a conference in Cambridge. We take the opportunity to visit Berlin once more, staying with my beloved friends Konrad and Gaby, who Jeanette will meet at last. We travel to Hamburg to stay with Manuel and his family, exploring the city, seeking out places where Lily and Carl may have lived. It's lovely to spend this time with my helpers; without them, we would never have got this far. Returning to Berlin, we visit bookshops and cafés, but the sweetest moment of all is high tea at the Hotel Adlon. This is the same hotel – rebuilt post-war – where, in 1940, my great-uncle Uly sat down with Luftwaffe General Ernst Udet, whose airforce would soon be fighting the Battle of Britain. The tea and the cakes were superb, as was the young waiter, who listened patiently to my story of why we were in Berlin. He was more than a credit to this historic establishment, poor man.

The end of our stay in Berlin is a time for final visits to galleries and of course, the inimitable Hauskonzerte taking place regularly in the Kutt household. These new friends have proved to me again and again that history has no inevitable outcome in relationships, if hearts and minds remain open.

Hotel Adlon, Berlin, 2015: afternoon tea time with Uncle Uly's ghost.

Back in London I find my way to the place in Green Lanes, Islington, N16, where Lily lived post-war with that household of a dozen German women, some perhaps, like her, in no hurry at all to return to a bombed, ruined Germany, where homes and families were uprooted – or vanished. Now the moment has come: the pilgrimage to Kensal Green Cemetery in West London to find the graves of Lily's son Carl and his wife, Irma. This is to be our final act, among all these searches in the north. From there, it will have to be more detective work back home, still trying to make sense of what's been revealed, digging deeper into the lives of these Nazi family ghosts of mine – welcome or not.

The grave of Carl Ulysses Hasenburg, Kensal Green Cemetery, London, 2015.

On July the 27th, by tube and train to Kensal Green Station in Brent, West London, we go, to the nearby Cemetery of All Souls. I know that somewhere there are the graves of Carl Hasenburg the younger and Irma, his German wife. Ashes Plot 62579/224/64: such a cold title for the final resting place, but without it we'd be wandering around here for hours. With the help of a sexton who was cleaning the graves, we come to the place where all of this searching was leading me: an area of London not so far from where my dad was born in Hammersmith, and me in Kingston-on-Thames, half an hour north. It's a kind of family gathering of the missing, who never knew how close they were and how close they came. Here you are, Carl, here at last you really are. Or really were. It's hard to know just what is real now, standing here, looking down.

The buried ashes of Lily's son Carl was as close as I would ever get to her, she whose bones were long ago burned, her ashes scattered. I sat there for a very long time in silence, wondering what might have been, had I known back in 1987 what I knew now. That one missed chance to meet Carl and Irma, when we had landed, uprooted, from

Memorial, Irma and Carl Hasenburg, Kensal Green Cemetery, London, 2015.

our New Zealand home. There would have been much emotion there, I dreamed, and many stories: long looks for resemblances, questions and answers, photographs shown, exchange of addresses, promises to meet again, and tears, yes, tears, us all embracing. It would have been as if my Nanny had brought forth a resurrection of sorts, all arising from those few cryptic entries in my aunt Lillian's tiny 1934 diary, the address book that told me where to find Lily and Carl Hasenburg in their Hamburg home. Now, there was the earth, and the grass, birds, and my breathing – better than nothing, of course. So much better than nothing.

But where was Irma? I looked around, then spied at the foot of Carl's plot something shiny in the grass. There she was, a small plaque laid at his feet, in memory of them both: 'Mr and Mrs Hasenburg. RIP'. I saw that there were fresh flowers, 'For Mr and Mrs Hasenburg'. The sexton told us, 'Yes, there was someone there, recently . . .' – but of course, there was no name, no way of finding out, save by staking out the grave and waiting. Whoever they were, what if they came back only once a year, for an anniversary? It was nearly thirty years

At the graves of Carl and Irma Hasenburg, Kensal Green Cemetery, London, 2015.

since these deaths in London – so who was this? They may as well be ghosts. Our time in the city was coming to an end; no way now to find this spirit. This is war, migration, this is time itself, the losing of our relatives. My Nanny never quite lost them: if only Mum, when Nanny died, had found Carl's letters. Did she?

What was I left with, sitting there, at the end of this search for the missing? Was it all about the quest; was having these encounters a goal in itself, as much as finding out more about my lost ones? What about my new relations in the wider world: Kate, Konrad, Gaby, Manuel and many others who had helped me and, in the process, had become real friends, had become whānau in the present? For the dead, no help is possible. What about all these new relationships, found and made real in the journey of the search, all of them joining me now, as my living human family? One such friend made on the road is Diana Wichtel, author of that heart-breaking masterpiece of Shoah pilgrimage, *Driving to Treblinka* – the search for her lost father and his final resting place.[1] With her years spent as a journalist, she has created a work of literary art from material that could have drowned a sentimentalist. I confess, the pilgrimage captured had me in tears, experiencing kinship with the heart of her search. So many hard-won insights could be quoted from Diana's book. Let this stand: the discovery of her great-aunt, Sabina, mother of her cousin Joe, also discovered. 'I was thirty two when she died. I could have met her if only I'd known. If I wanted to drive myself crazy that's one of the things I think about. Chasing the past is a recurring bad dream, the kind where you get there just too late.'[2] Carl and Irma. The lost.

HOME

CODA

The Real Story of the Book

How Uly Springs Lily from Germany, 1940–41

Much later than this, several years later, in fact, I'm still trying to untangle the web. By thought unbidden it seems, walking the dog, all of this comes to me. Question: what is the real story of the book, in a sentence?

In WW2, a brother gets his sister out of Nazi Germany.

How does he do this? By his imposture as an American journalist in early 1940 and, later, by the story he tells of 'her marriage to a murdered Jew'. It's not true. It's theatre.

How does this work? Who helps Uly? Remember that he meets Ernst Udet, the Luftwaffe chief and Great War flying ace, who was second only to Manfred von Richthofen (the Red Baron). They spend time together in the posh Hotel Adlon (yes, the aforementioned).

Why would Udet meet an American journalist in 1940? Udet *loves* meeting (and impressing) foreigners. He is a cosmopolitan bon vivant, and of course he's going to talk to Uly in 1940, in the swanky Adlon. He's not your average stupid Nazi ideologue. 'American journalist meets Fighter Ace' – this is the script here.

So what? Here is a contact making it possible for Uly to appeal to Udet for help in getting his sister 'back home' to England? Udet could swing it, easily, and he's quite comfortable with wining and dining foreign newspaper men. By this time in 1940, he's also not in love with bossy Göring – another Great War fighter ace and a confirmed drug addict, somewhat obese by now, not listening to anyone's advice.

Any other proof? Well, not exactly evidence, but as mentioned earlier – citing Captain Eric Brown's memoir, *Wings on My Sleeve* – Udet has form. Brown, a wartime Fleet Air Arm pilot officer and later test pilot, had met Udet twice before the war. In this account, he notes how eager Udet was to interact with and impress foreigners. On one occasion, in 1936, he flew the young Brown inverted in a stunt biplane, a few metres above the tarmac, then looped it, prior to landing.[1]

Helpers? Uly's son John is working as an American diplomat in the Swiss Embassy in Bern. He would have helped his father get his sister (John's aunt) out of Hamburg. Uly was already a practised liar and an experienced diplomat, who had served in Germany before the First World War. Uly – perhaps with John's help – made up this story about the 'murdered Jewish husband' to get this Englishwoman, his sister Lily, out of Germany and into England via the Swiss Embassy, sometime between mid 1940 and mid 1941.

What about Robin Bywater and the 'Jewish husband'? Let's say Uly told his nephew Robin what would later become the 'Aunt Lily's murdered Jewish husband story'. This was what Robin told me. Why would Uly tell him a lie? To keep things consistent. Wouldn't he want everybody in England to be hearing the same story? Once Lily gets to London, it becomes clear there never was 'a Jewish husband' (we find her German husband, Carl Hasenburg – who was not a Jew – was interned for the duration of the war, in Canada).

Carl returns to Germany in 1945. The place he goes back to is not a devastated Hamburg, but Wuppertal – to Hagen, not far from his birthplace in Radevormwald – where he starts a new life. He seems to have had some kind of relationship with another woman, Emily Böhmer (a friend? his landlady?). He dies in 1954, a few years after

Lily. His friendly landlady is a witness on his death certificate. Lily is named as Carl's late wife on his death certificate, just as he was named as her husband on hers.

Did Lily's son Carl attend his mother's funeral in Germany in 1951? You would think so – after all, his father was still alive. We have already seen how it was certain that Carl, Irma and Lily would be reunited, in postwar London. There's also good reason to think that Carl would have seen his mother Lily in 1943, when his sister Anita died in Liverpool.

By the time of Great-aunt Lily's death in 1951, my grandmother was with us in Auckland. She knew of her sister's death, I'm sure. Their brother Uly knew; and he would at least have written to tell her the news. She had his last address in England, before his death in 1961. They would still have been in touch.

Somehow, while regaling me with many stories, neither Nanny nor my mother mentioned anything of this to me in my teenage years. I was nineteen when Nanny Eunice died in 1967. It wasn't as if I was still a child and couldn't understand.

We know that when Nanny came to New Zealand, she had Carl junior's address. She must have been in contact. Carl and Irma are both alive in 1987, when we land in London. He dies in December; Irma early in 1988. I have since discovered that probate on Carl's estate was given early in the years of the new millennium – but to whom? Nobody can tell me.

Finally, in 2015, those flowers on the graves, visited, the sexton said, quite recently. By who? No clue: and as there seem to be no other witnesses – at least those I could have contacted, but was unable to find – I have to rest my case. Let the dead lie in peace. May any reader who has been gracious enough to follow me in my searching now also rest.

POSTSCRIPT

Germany After 1945

It may seem to any reader, come this far, that we know very little of Lily Hasenburg the person, who grew up with my grandmother, getting into childhood games and tricks such as climbing out of the bedroom window in Liverpool, shinnying up the gas streetlights and putting them out as the gas lighter moved along the street; or down in the cellar, shooting at a bullseye target with a Derringer pistol their father had brought home from America for his children. Then there was that stuffed grizzly bear in the lounge, brought back from Papa's escapades in the wilds of America – a creature mounted upright in attack mode on its hind legs, that would terrify unwary new maids entering the room, causing some to resign on the spot. And of course, we have the wonderful Buffalo Bill story, recounted earlier.

But of Lily, of her actual voice, there exists only that one quote from Eunice, my grandmother, of Lily enthusing over Adolf Hitler, back in 1934. How am I then willing to write of a woman – of whom we know so very little – as my 'Nazi aunt'? We do know that she accepted money from Hitler's government while interned on the Isle of Man during the war. Does that make her complicit? Jewish women internees refused.

When Lily finally did return to Germany for the last three years of her life, she had missed the early desperate days of defeat, from April 1945 until 1948. As Harald Jähner writes in *Aftermath*, there were 'those who had lost their children while fleeing and were relentlessly in search of them; sick people who, for want of proper medical help, faded for months between life and death; the traumatised who had lost the will to live; and, finally, people for whom, after the end of the war, every laughing face looked like a mocking grimace'.[1] German memoirist Rolf Panny, who grew up in the same era as Lily lived through, has written a first-hand account of his postwar experiences in a broken, defeated Germany. In May 1947, on a visit as a prentice journalist to Dortmund, laid waste by Allied bombing, he met some of those left behind and marooned by the tides of war. In the basement of his hotel (all the upper floors had been destroyed), he met two Polish POWs who had been made slave labourers as farm workers by the Nazis. Serge and Josef needed a clearance from the new Polish government to return home, but their villages were gone, wiped out in the war.

That night Panny wrote up this chance meeting, wondering 'about the suffering of untold numbers of foreigners, forced to work in German armament factories or on the land; they were now stateless and lived in the illusion of freedom without the prospect of ever finding a home in a destroyed Europe'.[2] Two days later, after visiting town planners with no town left, but tasked to plan anew among the ruins, he walked the streets, notepad and pencil at the ready, to ask locals he met about their town.

> Not many were willing to answer my questions. Most were glum. Elderly folk in rags were walking about aimlessly. They stared at me and shook their heads. Refugees from Eastern Germany said they were desperate to start a new life somewhere. They only wanted to talk about the homes they had to flee when the Russians came. Others were out hunting for food or searching for members of their families. Children in small gangs were climbing in and out of the ruins. How could I write a profile of a city that didn't exist any longer. I only heard people's cry for help.[3]

It is not surprising that Panny's feelings were unacceptable to Mr Friedlaender, back at the pages of *Die Zeit* in Hamburg: 'You should have left your emotions at home' was his cool response – ending a promising career. Fortunately for posterity, Rolf Panny's testimony has survived.

Whatever Lily experienced in London in those three years before her return to Germany, we can understand that it was nothing at all like the experience of the millions of displaced, homeless and bereaved hordes of humanity flooding Germany – those whom the Allies had to feed, house and, in the case of returning troops, imprison and process for possible war crimes. She had a sister – my grandmother – close by in London, and she had her brother Uly. There was also, of course, her Anglicised German-born son Carl junior, and his wife Irma. Is it any surprise that she chose to remain in her natal England, where she had lived out most of the war? She would also have avoided something far greater: facing the reality of what we know today as the Holocaust, and its German silence, seeing daily the ruin of her adopted country.

In 1949 the Jewish philosopher Hannah Arendt, forced from Germany in 1933, returned from her American exile as the director of the Jewish Cultural Reconstruction organisation, to report on the after-effects of Nazi rule. She wrote of a horrifying mental state that existed outside of Berlin; in the capital, she found some evidence of a hatred of Hitler, but elsewhere, there existed, 'a striking outward symptom of a deep-rooted, stubborn and sometimes brutal refusal to face up to what actually happened, and come to terms with it'.[4] On 25 November 1949 Wolfgang Hedler, a deputy in the Bundestag and a member of the far-right 'Deutsch Partei' (DP), opined on 'the fuss made of the use of gas to kill the Jews', when 'there might have been other ways of getting rid of them'. He was beaten up by deputies of the Social Democratic Party (SPD) and thrown out of his party, but covert Nazi comrades remained.[5] Later events such as the Auschwitz trials for the murder of millions did not begin until long after Lily and Carl's deaths. Whatever meetings they may have had with their own consciences, we will never know. Like all of those Germans – and non-Germans – who lived through the Hitler years, and made no known attempt to reject him and his regime, to that degree, Lily will always remain as my Nazi aunt. In a murderous dictatorship within its own borders, and a genocidal aggressor beyond them, they became complicit through the slow poisoning of acquiescence. Those who did resist paid with their lives.

Trains to Life, Trains to Death: bronze sculpture of Jewish child deportees by Frank Meisler, Friedrichstraße Bahnhof, Berlin (detail).

'The optimistically conceived phrase that life goes on is in fact a measure of the damnation of the world. Life goes on because human conscience is lifeless,' wrote Hans Habe in *Off Limits*, his novel of occupied Germany.[6] Lily was not able to speak to me. I'm almost certain that she never visited my mother, with us two little boys, in Kingston-on-Thames: she never saw me. If she had, Mum might have told me.

Yet Lily is speaking to me now, through this journey: seemingly eluding my efforts to find out more about her, to get closer than when we began. But she does have a final message, in spite of all: *don't turn your back on evil, nor take the Führer's coin.*

E te whaea kēkē nui, e te tuākana o tāku kuia, e Lily, haere atu rā, moe mai rā!

Lilian Edith Bywater, 1876–1951, passport photo, 1934.
ANCESTRY.COM, PUBLIC DOMAIN

Notes

In the Beginning, the Dead
1. Sarah Kafatou, 'An Interview with W.G. Sebald', *Harvard Review Online*, 8 December 2021; originally published in *Harvard Review* 15, Fall 1998.

Chapter 1: Listening to Nanny Eunice
1. Richard J. Evans, *The Coming of the Third Reich*, Penguin, London, 2004, p. 72.
2. From Ship's Manifest: SS *Ivernia*, Liverpool – Boston, 30 November 1909: 'Bywater, Peter Daniel, 61, Rubber stamp maker, Born USA, soldier in Civil War, Country – USA, Philadelphia, Daughter Eunice Bywater, Cheltenham, Final destination – [unclear on document]'. From 'List or Manifest of Alien Passengers For the United States', sourced on Ancestry.com.
3. https://liverpoolhiddenhistory.co.uk/when-buffalo-bill-came-to-newsham-park/
4. William H. Honan, *Bywater: The Man Who Invented the Pacific War*, Macdonald, London, 1990, p. 9 – an account of the life of Bywater's youngest son Hector, which mentions details of the father's early peripatetic life. See also William H. Honan, *Visions of Infamy*, St Martin's Press, New York, 1991, p. 5, where Honan adds the information about Bywater's friendship with Cody. The William F. Cody Archive has a link displaying an account from the *Liverpool Courier* newspaper of 13 July 1891, on the Cody show display at Newsham Park: 'The Wild West Show', https://codyarchive.org/texts/wfc.nsp11529.html
5. I have tracked down Eunice's application for US citizenship. It seems the Bywaters were good at this, riding on their Welsh father's Civil War record, and honorary US citizenship. Ulysses did the same thing, faking his US citizenship while working at the US Consulate in Dresden.
6. John Tenniel Cartoon, *Punch*, 1896.09.05.115. There are many versions of this rhyme: see the image at http://punch.photoshelter.com/image/I0000Vu8Ftf8_58Y

Chapter 2: Meeting the Remarkable Bywaters
1. Honan, *Bywater*, pp. 27–28.
2. Copy of original sighted, available in Ancestry.com.
3. Honan, *Bywater*, pp. 27–28.
4. Document copy in possession of the author.
5. Honan, *Bywater*, pp. 27–28.
6. See Jeffrey Paparoa Holman, *The Lost Pilot*, Penguin New Zealand, Auckland, 2013, p. 100, where I expand on Bywater's life and achievements in my account of Japan's rise to become a great naval power, as part of

a history of the kamikaze attack on my father's aircraft carrier, HMS *Illustrious*, 6 April 1945, and tracing the aircrew's families in Japan. See also H.C. Bywater and H.C. Ferraby, *Strange Intelligence: Memoirs of Naval Secret Service*, Constable & Co., London, 1930: in Chapter IX, Bywater writes of 'a former member of the [Secret] Service' whose pre-war espionage activities in German naval yards gave priceless information to the British – Bywater himself.
7 Ulysses Bywater died on 12 August, 1961, in Bournemouth, as noted by me in Stanza XVII of Tennyson's *In Memoriam*, my aunt Lillian's copy, given to me by my grandmother in 1966, the year before she died.
8 Of this journey of Uly's to Germany in 1940, more will follow.

Chapter 3: Cousin Robin and the Jewish Husband
1 Hector C. Bywater, *Their Secret Purposes: Dramas and Mysteries of the Naval War*, Constable, London, 1932; Hector C. Bywater, *The Great Pacific War: A History of the American–Japanese Campaign of 1931–33*, Constable, London, 1925.
2 All attempts to have the Red Cross authenticate this element of Robin's account have proved unsuccessful. Neither the US, the UK, nor the New Zealand Red Cross have found material here. Uly did go to Germany in 1940 and Lily did get to England, as we will see.
3 I refer to the diary as 'my grandmother's' here, but she was in fact using her late daughter Lillian's diary, a tiny book she had taken over early in the year, as Lillian's condition worsened. More on this to come.

Chapter 4: Nanny's Address Book and Mormon Helpers
1 A.R.D. Fairburn, 'The Voyage' (for Philip Smithells), 1952. https://www.nzepc.auckland.ac.nz/authors/fairburn/voyage.asp
2 'Now if there is no resurrection, what will those do who are baptised for the dead? If the dead are not raised at all, why are people baptised for them?' 1 Corinthians 15:29, NIV, Zondervan, Grand Rapids, Michigan, 1984.
3 See Peter Gillman and Leni Gillman, *'Collar the Lot': How Britain Interned and Expelled its Wartime Refugees*, Quartet, London, 1980.

Chapter 6: Germany is My Teacher
1 Otto Dov Kulka: *Landscapes of the Metropolis of Death*, Penguin, London, 2014.
2 Ibid., p. 80.

Chapter 8: Encounters in London Fields
1 'Negative capability' – a term coined by the poet John Keats, described as 'being in uncertainties, mysteries, doubts, without any irritable reaching after fact and reason'. Letter to George and Tom Keats, 21,?27 December 1817, https://poetryfoundation.org/articles/69384/selections-from-keatss-letters
2 It is ten years since these diary notes were first written. A headstone has now been arranged. Along with his military history, and a copy of the medallion

Chapter 9: Manuel is My Hamburg Genealogist

1. Volker Ullrich, trans. Jefferson Chase, *Germany 1923: Hyperinflation, Hitler's Putsch and Democracy in Crisis*, Liveright, New York, 2023.
2. Jennifer Szalai, '*Germany 1923*: When democracy held Nazism at bay', book review, *New York Times*, 27 September 2023.
3. Some of these details have been added subsequently to the 2014 travel diary entries.

Chapter 10: Grunewald and the Leaping Hare

1. https://www.spiegel.de/international/germany/death-toll-debate-how-many-died-in-the-bombing-of-dresden-a-581992.html. The number of deaths has been the subject of intense debate ever since. In 2008 the Dresden Commission of Historians arrived at the figure of 18,000–25,000.
2. The V-1 was a pulse-jet pilotless flying bomb, capable of up to 600kph; the V-2 rocket was the world's first long-range ballistic missile, impossible to intercept, or detect, once launched. These launch sites were finally overrun by the advancing Allies, but not before 2754 civilians had been killed in London and over 6000 injured.

Chapter 11: Taking Old Glory Back to Dresden

1. Kurt Tucholsky, *Berlin! Berlin! Dispatches from the Weimar Republic*, Berlinica Publishing, Berlin, 2017.

Chapter 13: Victor Culture and Colonial Amnesia

1. https://www.liverpoolecho.co.uk/news/liverpool-news/hitler-stay-liverpool-citys-fascinating-12366612. The Hitler family address was only five kilometres from my grandmother's home in Wavertree, a fifteen-minute journey by car today. Irony of ironies.
2. NZ History, 'New Zealand in Sāmoa: Black Saturday'. https://nzhistory.govt.nz/politics/samoa/black-saturday
3. See 'Hitler's debt to America', extract from Edwin Black, *War Against the Weak: Eugenics and America's Campaign to Create a Master Race*, Turnaround, London, 2004: reproduced in the *Guardian*, 6 February 2004, https://www.theguardian.com/uk/2004/feb/06/race.usa
4. See Oliver Sutherland, *Paikea: The Life of I.L.G. Sutherland*, Canterbury University Press, Christchurch, 2013; see also Jules Older, 'Every New Zealander should know the Sutherlands', *The Spinoff*, 13 January 2023, https://thespinoff.co.nz/summer-2022/13-01-2023/every-new-zealander-should-know-the-sutherlands-2
5. Robert Graves, *Goodbye to All That*, Cassell, London, 1957, p. 60.
6. Ibid. The Pour le Mérite (or 'Blue Max') was a military order of merit established by Frederick II of Prussia.

Chapter 14: English Lily in a German War

1. See Matthew Stibbe, *British Civilian Internees in Germany: The Ruhleben Camp, 1914–1918*, Manchester University Press, Manchester, 2008, chapter 1, 'The politics of alien internment Germany', pp. 25–44. As noted above, there is no proof that Lily was interned; this text gives a background.
2. Modris Eksteins, *Rites of Spring: The Great War and the Birth of the Modern Age*, Mariner Books, Boston, 2000, pp. 56, 62.
3. See Adam Hochschild, *To End All Wars: A Story of Loyalty and Rebellion, 1914–1918*, Mariner Books, New York, 2012, pp. 215–17, 311–13.

Chapter 15: Great-uncle Uly and the Gestapo

1. The following quotes from *Weltwoche* and the Swiss police report, Bern, 1940, come from material provided by Swiss archivists in Bern, via the Swiss Embassy in Berlin (documents in the author's possession).
2. International Committee of the Red Cross, Attestation, received from Geneva, 21 October 2015.
3. Text in this article has been translated with the assistance of Tanja Schwalm.
4. This is referring to Lily Hasenburg, his sister in Hamburg.
5. Copy in author's possession from Swiss Government Archives, in Bern.
6. Ulysses' son John Bywater was the US consul there. In the middle of a war, it appears Uly was visiting family.
7. The Swiss police can't prove that Ulysses was the author of the article in German, published in the Swiss newspaper *Die Weltwoche*, but it would be a breach of his conditions if he were being paid for it. See previous note and image that follows here. Copies in the author's possession.
8. '"Je Reviens d'Allemagne", par un observateur neutre', *Paris-soir*, 27 January 1940, n.p. Copy in author's collection.
9. See Eric Brown, *Wings on My Sleeve*, Weidenfeld & Nicholson, London, 2006, pp. 7–9. Captain Brown, a test pilot, met Udet twice before WW2.
10. Stephen Spender, *World Within World: The Autobiography of Stephen Spender*, Readers Union, London, 1953, p. 91.

Chapter 16: Lily is Interned on the Isle of Man

1. Information provided in material copied and forwarded by the Swiss Archives, Bern.
2. Home Office letter to Swiss Legation, London, I/GEN 3/11.1, 4th August 1941. Author's emphasis.
3. All copies of the following correspondence were obtained from Swiss Archives, Bern, sighted, and now in the possession of the author.
4. See Yvonne M. Cresswell (ed.), *Living with the Wire: Civilian Internment in the Isle of Man during the Two World Wars*, Manx National Heritage, 1994. The following information on life in the camps is from here.
5. Anita, Lily Hasenburg's daughter, moved to England sometime after the Great War, as had her older brother, Carl. She married Christopher Fincken in Liverpool in 1937, aged twenty-nine.
6. The following ICRC records were forwarded to me in 2015, in response

Chapter 17: Looking into the Graves

1. Dr. Jeffrey Paparoa Holman, a writer and historian from Christchurch in New Zealand, is asking for help in finding information about his great aunt, whose husband came from the Wuppertal area. He writes: "My English great aunt Lilian Edith Bywater married Carl Hasenburg in Liverpool in 1898. He was born in Önkfeld in 1874 and died in Wuppertal in 1954. Before that he lived in Hagen; my great aunt, who died before him, also lived there. I hope to get in touch with relatives of the Hasenburgs who can help me with information about Carl and his wife."

   Dr. Holman can be contacted at the following email address ...
2. Julia Boyd, *Travellers in the Third Reich*, Elliott & Thompson, London, 2017, p. 25.
3. Ibid., p. 37.
4. Spender, *World Within World*; letter to Isaiah Berlin 30.1.1930.
5. Ibid., p. 99.
6. Simone Weil, 'The Situation in Germany', in *Formative Writings 1929–1941*, ed. and trans. D.T. McFarland and W. Van Ness, University of Massachusetts Press, Amherst, 1987, p. 97.
7. Wolfram Eilenberger, *The Visionaries: Arendt, Beauvoir, Rand, Weil and the Salvation of Philosophy*, Allen Lane/Penguin Random House UK, London, 2023, p. 41.
8. Weil, 'The Situation in Germany' (author's emphasis).
9. Lily Hasenburg's death certificate (author's translation).
10. Carl Hasenburg's death certificate (trans. Manuel Petzold).

Chapter 18: From the Hotel Adlon to Kensal Green

1. Diana Wichtel, *Driving to Treblinka: A Long Search for a Lost Father*, Awa Press, Wellington, 2017.
2. Ibid., p. 125.

Coda: The Real Story of the Book

1. Brown, *Wings on My Sleeve*, pp. 7–9.

Postscript: Germany after 1945

1. Harald Jähner, *Aftermath: Life in the Fallout of the Third Reich, 1945–1955*, Vintage, New York, 2023, p. 92.
2. Rolf Panny, *Between Hitler & a Hard Place: A Memoir 1924–1948*, Steele Roberts Aotearoa, Wellington, 2011, p. 251.
3. Ibid., p. 253.
4. Hannah Arendt, 'The Aftermath of Nazi Rule: Report from Germany' (essay), in *Commentary*, vol. 10, 1 January 1950, New York, 1950, pp. 342–53.
5. Jähner, *Aftermath*, pp. 319–20.
6. Hans Habe, trans. Ewald Osers, *Off Limits: A Novel of Occupied Germany*, George G. Harrap, London, 1956, p. 119.

Bibliography

Anon, trans. Alcuin, *I Saw Poland Suffer,* by a Polish Doctor, Lindsay Drummond, London, 1941.
Bessel, Richard, *Germany After the First World War*, Clarendon Press, Oxford, 1993.
Bible, New International Version, Zondervan, Grand Rapids, 1984.
Black, Edwin, *War Against the Weak: Eugenics and America's Campaign to Create a Master Race*, Turnaround, London, 2004.
Boyd, Julia, *Travellers in the Third Reich*, Elliott & Thompson, London, 2017.
Bywater, Ulysses, 'Je Reviens d'Allemagne', *Paris-soir*, 27 January 1940.
Cresswell, Yvonne M. (ed.), *Living with the Wire: Civilian Internment in the Isle of Man during the Two World Wars*, Manx National Heritage, Douglas, Isle of Man, 2010.
Eilenberger, Wolfgang, *The Visionaries: Arendt, Beauvoir, Rand, Weil and the Salvation of Philosophy*, Allen Lane/Penguin Random House UK, London, 2023.
Eksteins, Modris, *Rites of Spring: The Great War and the Birth of the Modern Age*, Mariner Books, Boston, 2000.
Evans, Richard J., *The Coming of the Third Reich*, Penguin, London, 2004.
Flanagan, Richard, *Question 7*, Knopf/Penguin Random House, Australia, 2023.
Gillman, Peter and Leni Gillman, *'Collar the Lot': How Britain Interned and Expelled its Wartime Refugees*, Quartet, London, 1980.
Graves, Robert, *Goodbye to All That*, Cassell, London, 1957.
Green, William, *Famous Fighters of the Second World War*, Macdonald, London, 1957.
Grunberger, Richard, *A Social History of the Third Reich*, Phoenix, London, 2005.
Hochschild, Adam, *To End All Wars: A Story of Loyalty and Rebellion, 1914–1918*, Mariner Books, New York, 2012.
Honan, William H., *Bywater: The Man Who Invented the Pacific War*, Macdonald, London, 1990.
Jähner, Harald, *Aftermath: Life in the Fallout of the Third Reich, 1945–1955*, Vintage, New York, 2023; English translation, Shaun Whiteside, 2021.
Kulka, Otto Dov, *Landscapes of the Metropolis of Death*, Penguin, London, 2014.
MacGregor, Neil, *Germany: Memories of a Nation*, Penguin Random House, London, 2014.
Panny, Rolf, *Between Hitler & a Hard Place: A Memoir 1924–1948*, Steele Roberts Aotearoa, Wellington, 2011.
Parkin, Simon, *The Island of Extraordinary Captives: A True Story of an Artist, a Spy and a Wartime Scandal*, Sceptre, London, 2022.
Rilke, Rainer Maria, trans. Edward Snow, *The Book of Images*, North Point Press, Berkeley, 1994.

Spender, Stephen, *World Within World: The Autobiography of Stephen Spender*, Readers Union, London, 1953.
Stibbe, Matthew, *British Civilian Internees in Germany: The Ruhleben Camp, 1914–1918*, Manchester University Press, Manchester, 2008.
Sutherland, Oliver, *Paikea: The Life of I.L.G. Sutherland*, Canterbury University Press, Christchurch, 2013.
Taylor, A.J.P., *The First World War: An Illustrated History*, Hamish Hamilton, London, 1963.
Towey, Peter, *How to Research Your German Ancestors*, Anglo-German Family History Society, Wales, 2013.
Ullrich, Volker, trans. Jefferson Chase, *Germany 1923: Hyperinflation, Hitler's Putsch and Democracy in Crisis*, Liveright, New York, 2023.
Wichtel, Diana, *Driving to Treblinka: A Long Search for a Lost Father*, Awa Press, Wellington, 2017.

Mihimihi / Acknowledgements

Whānau: I acknowledge my family and close relatives
My grandmother, Eunice Winifred Airey, née Bywater.
My father, William Thomas (Bill) Holman and my mother, Mary Elisabeth Holman, née Woollam.
My brother, Eric Holman, and my late sisters, Jill Clarke and Elisabeth Richards.
Grateful thanks to Eric and his wife, Nancy, for support in remembering my grandfather with his new memorial.
My son Timothy Holman, his wife Cecile Aubert-Jacquin, Den Haag, and my grandsons, Samuel and Matthew.
My daughter Raine Rasala and her husband, Scott, Danville CA, and my granddaughters, Madelaine and Kate.
Theresa Newcombe, mother of our children, and Alice Noble, their Nana.
My wife Jeanette King.
Adele and Mark Sissons.
The late Reverend Robin Bywater, whānau.
Pat Snow, my dear, late English aunt.

Friends: helpers, teachers, readers, publishers
The late Bill Honan, author, friend.
Professor Patrick Evans, supporter, encourager, editor.
Staff, English Programme, University of Canterbury.
Norma Orlowski, night school teacher, Hagley College.
Konrad and Gaby Kutt, my Berlin hosts, whānau.
Kate Karle, helper, friend, Christchurch and Hamburg.
Britta Groeger, helper, friend, Berlin.
Staff of the Goethe-Institut, Berlin.
Staff of the Goethe-Institut, Neuseeland.
Nicole Brauer, meine Deutschlehrerin, Goethe-Institut, Berlin.
Classmates of 2014, Goethe-Institut, Berlin.
Manuel Petzold, genealogist, pou whare, Hamburg: this book could not have succeeded without you, mein wunderbarer Familienhistoriker.
Helena, his partner, and their daughter, Luise.
Elke Rosin, legend, Berlin.
Kate and the late Tony Grant, Selsey.
Rainer and Alexandra Gotthardt, Grunewald.
Vera Leier, University of Canterbury German teacher, adviser.
Tanja Schwalm, translator.
Swiss Embassy, Berlin.
Swiss Government archivists, Bern.
Holger Starke, Stadtmuseum archivist, Dresden.

Roger Steele, Steele Roberts Aotearoa, rangatira.
Chris Harvey, tōhunga tā moko, mauri ora!
Margaret Samuels, long-time whānau, PR maven.
Diana Wichtel, writer, fellow pilgrim.
Catherine and Katrina, Canterbury University Press, my publishing and editorial team.
Gillian Tewsley, Pepperleaf Publishing, my eagle-eyed editor.
Katrina Duncan, our book designer par excellence.
Luke and colleagues at Photo Warehouse, Fitzgerald Avenue, Christchurch, for work on the digital images of the Dresden chapter.
Last, not least, Mr Foxy-Jack Russell Hari, who took me walking on sanity-saving strolls.